A PARENT'S GUIDE TO
ROWING

A PARENT'S GUIDE TO
ROWING

HARRY BANNING LLOYD

APG

Dedicated to rowers and their coaches: we have spent time with them on the water, in the launch and on the riverbank and have been truly humbled by the experience.

Published by APG
Summerside House
Summerside
Buckland
Oxfordshire
SN7 8QW

Jacket photography by Matthew Morgan
Illustrations by Ruth Murray

Designed by Isobel Gillan
Printed and bound in Great Britain by Hunts – people in print, Oxford. www.hunts.co.uk

Efforts have been made to obtain all necessary permission to reproduce quoted material. Any errors or omissions should be notified to the publisher and will be corrected in future editions.

Cataloguing in Publication Data is available from the British Library.

ISBN: 978-0-9563675-0-1

CONTENTS

'Rowing – it's only a boat and two oars, why does it take up so much of our lives?'

ELIZA, A NON-ROWER, AGED 9

'Rowing is a bit like childbirth. You forget the pain and come back and do it again …'

SUE BROWN (X PRESS BOAT CLUB AND REGULAR FISA WORLD MASTER MEDAL WINNER) 'ROWING & REGATTA', ISSUE 27, AUGUST 08

FOREWORD

There is no doubt about the fact that rowing is addictive. If your children have been involved for a while then this is something that I'm sure you already know, if not then it won't take you long to find out! It's a pretty time consuming activity, but the rewards go so far beyond the results on the water. My best school friendships were formed through the boat club, and these remain strong years after leaving. Rowing is a sport where success often comes more from hard work rather than natural talent, and the sense of pride in your achievements is incredibly rewarding.

A guide like this one would have been a huge help to my parents over the years. I have no doubt that without their unwavering support I would not have been able to realise my dreams. As their previous experiences of rowing extended only to watching the university boat races, and perhaps a corporate trip to Henley Royal Regatta, it has been hard for them to fully understand much of what I have been doing over the last 12 years. I'd like to think that now I'm a little bit more patient at explaining things but I know that, as a teenager, I didn't have much time to help them out, and confusion between sculling and rowing, head races and regattas and fours and quads was commonplace. As for trying to explain seat racing, I'm pretty sure I never even tried! This book will be useful to you whether you're a complete newcomer or a seasoned supporter, and you may even be tempted to give rowing a try yourself!

KATIE GREVES

Rowed for GB at Junior, U23 and Senior levels.
Rowed in GB Women's eight at 2008 Olympic Games.
Training for 2012 Olympics

Secret diary of a rowing slave

TIME 6.30 am
DATE Friday 23 May
EVENT National Schools Regatta
STATUS half way up the M1 with contents of my kitchen in the estate car
HAIR unbrushed mop
CAFFEINE two double espressos already

This is it. Culmination of the previous week's frantic preparation. Girls set off to the Regatta yesterday. Meeting up at 7.30 am to set up marquee and organise food. Previous experience of tents limited to wrestling with Wendy house in the garden — could be quite a challenge. Executive planning would put NATO to shame. Confident all potential eventualities of teenage tantrums, weather and squad's dietary requirements covered.

Smug complacency suddenly shattered. Look down and realise still wearing pyjama trousers. During car loading, had not wished to crease new cropped beige linen trousers and forgot to finish getting dressed. Suitcase with spare outfit is at bottom of mound of equipment in back of car. Despair.

INTRODUCTION

Rowing. It will give you laughter, tears, immense pride in your rower and amazing friendships. It is not only a hugely exciting sport but it is also complex. It can take years to row with good technique. There are books that can provide expert knowledge for your rower on how to achieve this. However, there is little information available about the sport that is aimed at parents.

If you have no experience of rowing yourself, you will soon find that your rower returns from training sessions talking about the sport in a language that you do not understand. He or she can very quickly become caught up in a sport about which you know very little.

This book aims to unravel this new language. It includes information for parents on what happens at training sessions, what rowers need for these sesssions, what happens before and during events, and how you will be involved with all of this. It gives advice on relevant health concerns and the impact rowing will have on your rower's school time and your family. It also provides information on the type of nutrition your teenage rower will need and gives ideas on how to incorporate this into both school and family life.

It ends with a section that provides factual information about rowing, so you will be able to join in with the chat about what is happening at competitions and training and also understand what your rower is going through.

This book is written by parents for parents. We hope that it might provide both informative and entertaining reading.

BOAT CLUBS

Your child's interest in rowing could have been ignited by one of the many inspirational rowers that Great Britain has seen over the years. They may be able to row for their school or for a boat club that has junior crews.

Rowing is a competitive sport and most schools and clubs aim to compete at the main junior rowing events in Great Britain at their level. The boys' main events in England are the Schools' Head of the River (Tideway), the Men's Head of the River, the Scullers Head of the River, the National Schools Regatta, the Henley Royal Regatta and the National Championships. For girls, the main events in England are the Schools' Head of the River (Tideway), the Women's Head of the River, the Scullers Head of the River, the National Schools Regatta, the Henley Women's Regatta and the National Championships. Strathclyde Park and the Scottish Championships are the main events in Scotland and the Welsh Open Rowing Championships is the main event for Wales.

FACT *The Leander Boat Club was founded in 1818 for men and is the first and most famous rowing club in the world. The first women's club was The Hammersmith Sculling Club for Girls, which was started by Dr Furnivall in 1896 when he wanted to promote the cause of women in rowing, having seen the poor health of the girls who served him tea in his favourite tea shop. The club now takes his name – The Furnivall Sculling Club.*
INFORMATION FROM: WWW.FURNIVALL.ORG

Many regattas, heads and indoor events take place in the different rowing regions – too numerous to list here. Your club will have a diary of the events for the year. Clubs vary in their ability to put together crews for all the junior age groups. A club may not be big enough or it may not have the aspirations or facilities to do this. It is worth finding out how seriously a club takes competitions and trying to find a club that has goals that match those of your child. If your child prefers to row for fun alone, it would be better to join a club that supports this, rather than one that focuses on medals.

Some schools and clubs are able to compete at international level, entering competitions such as the Boston Head of the Charles in USA (the largest two-day rowing event in the world), the Canadian Henley, the Armada Cup in Switzerland and the Gent Regatta in Belgium. It may be that only the top crew from the club is able to do this, but it nevertheless gives something for the younger rowers to aspire to.

'It wasn't only victories we experienced. All the outstanding coaches were building winning individuals for the competition of life.' J.J. FORSTER FORMER US OLYMPIC ROWER, AND COACH GEORGETOWN ROWING ASSOCIATION, USA

Some clubs may also offer an exchange programme with overseas clubs. This enables them to reciprocate hospitality and facilities. This is not only hugely rewarding but it also means that clubs can borrow boats and facilities when they visit abroad.

Your club or school may have a few members who row or have rowed for Great Britain at the J16, J18 and U23 ages. This would be at yearly events such as the World Rowing Junior Championships, the Coupe de la Jeunesse, the Home Countries or the Anglo-French Match. The Australian Youth Olympic Festival takes place in Sydney every two years. The Youth Olympic Games, held for the first time in 2010, has rowing as part of the Summer Games. These games occur every four years.

Most schools and clubs allow children to start sculling from the age of 11 and sweeping from the age of 14. It can be difficult to judge how promising your rower will be until after this age (J14) and until they have stopped growing. Some rowers flourish at university rather than at school. This means hours of training and early starts at weekends for rowers, parents and coaches alike, before the rower reaches his or her full potential.

The coaches at schools or clubs are typically dedicated and work long and often antisocial hours. It may be a hobby outside of a demanding job. They usually have a great deal of experience. Many are rowers themselves and have switched to coaching and completed British Rowing training courses. It is only through their dedication and commitment that your rower will achieve.

Rowing is not like other sports where parents can sit and watch training sessions and listen to the advice that their child is receiving. This is because parents of rowers are generally banned from the indoor training sessions and on the water the crews row past at great speed. It can be difficult to get to know the coaches and to feel part of things. One of the ways you can do this is to become involved in the club.

Depending upon your available time and interest, you could offer to:

- provide lifts to and from events and training
- provide and sometimes serve food at both
- provide hospitality to other rowers
- act as the parent representative for your rower's year group
- join the Rowing Committee and help with fund raising
- marshal or coach (after appropriate training!).

Secret diary of a rowing slave

TIME 6.30 am
DATE Saturday 12 December
SITE snug under duvet in bed
AIR TEMPERATURE minus 2 centigrade
STATUS barely awake
HAIR covered in traditional Nepalese Sherpa headgear
CAFFEINE unavailable

Alarm clock shatters my dreams. Offer to pick up rest of the crew and take to the river smashes into reality. Training starts at 8 am. Head muzzy from Pinot Grigio last night. Why isn't the central heating on? It is on, but absolutely freezing outside. 1 cm of ice on windscreen of car. Girls descend slowly downstairs. Interrogation about lack of suitable kit met with a grunt. Squeal pierces the silence when I inadvertently fill the water flask without enough juice in it. Reprimanded for attempting to pack bags. Rebuffed when suggest that waterproofs a good idea.

File outside, unable to find de-icer. Try hot water to melt the ice before resorting to scraping windscreen with daughter's nail file. Snap two finger nails. Crawl down drive with my nose on windscreen. Lean forward to peer through small orifice in the ice. Hold my breath to prevent glasses steaming up. Collect rest of crew who sit silently abreast before daughter remarks 'Don't worry about my mum – she can drive really.'

TRAINING

Each boat club has different training demands depending on the age of the rower, his or her capability, the facilities of the club and the number of competitions that they enter. By the time your child reaches a top crew they will be training most days and will have training or events at weekends and in the school holidays. In this way, rowing has an impact on the entire family.

> **FACT** *Rowing uses all the major muscle groups in the body and nowadays rowers need to be supremely fit. Leading up to the 1908 Olympic Games, the rowers trained twice a day on weekdays, with a morning run and an evening row, and they did not train at weekends. For 2012, the GB team will train three times a day and will need to commit to hours of training each week with team GB.* INFORMATION FROM: WWW.INSPIREDBYROWING.ORG.UK

Most rowers train in order to be able to compete. Races are won and lost by fractions of a second. In order to win, a rower needs to be fit, skilful and mentally strong so that they can push themselves to their limit and continue pushing even when they want to stop.

Training is therefore both physical and mental and essentially covers the following areas:

- core stability
- flexibility
- technique
- endurance
- strength.

It is a continuous process and is important not only for fitness, but also for water safety and prevention of injuries. Rowers need to develop and maintain their flexibility and core stability in order to row correctly, without damaging themselves (their backs in particular). This is regardless of whether they are training competitively or rowing for fun. An example of a core stability exercise sheet is given in the appendix section.

All rowers need to approach their training with the right mental attitude. They need to be keen to learn and ready to listen to the instructions of the coaches. This is not always easy. However tempting it might be, skipping a lap or missing out a few push ups can make a difference in the end, either in the form of an injury or missing out on selection for a place in a boat. This motivation needs to come from the rower alone, as no matter how much you want your child to succeed, it is their determination and hard work that makes the difference. Being a 'PP' (pushy parent) doesn't really work.

'We do more before 8 am than most people do all day long …'

ANON. – HEARTFELT BY PARENTS AND ROWERS ALIKE

Indoor training

Rowers use some or all of the following pieces of equipment and methods of torture in their quest to fulfil their dreams and aspirations. The first two on the list are used to develop technique and endurance (an hour on the ergo for example). The rest of the list might form part of a circuit, where the rower does two minutes of each exercise, using maximum effort, and then moves to the next station. The number of times they do the routine is recorded ('reps').

Skipping ropes These are used at speed (e.g. five one minute bursts), which is more difficult and tiring than you might imagine.

Ergometers 'ergos' These are used to build up strength and technique. Novice rowers also use them to learn how to row.

FACT *Ergo is short for the word ergometer, which comes from the Greek words 'ergon' meaning 'work' and 'metron', meaning 'measure'. The first time the power output of a rower was recorded was in 1957. The first rowing machines were developed in 1900 in the USA, and the most commonly used Concept 2 was developed in 1981. This has revolutionised rowing training*
INFORMATION FROM: WWW.INSPIREDBYROWING.ORG.UK

Row perfect equipment This is different from an ergo machine as the feet, seat and screen move to simulate a boat on water. Ergo machines can also be moved onto special tracks to have the same effect.

Dyno equipment This is used to test three things: leg push away strength, arm pull strength and arm push away strength.

Pull up bar This helps rowers to develop upper body strength. They hang suspended from the bar and then try to pull themselves up above the bar.

Weights/bench press They will push up weights whilst lying on the floor.

Stability balls These are used for core stability and balance work.

Spinning bicycles These are regarded as pure torture and are used to build up endurance. Rowers set the resistance on the machines and then cycle at speed for varying distances or times. They are very tiring and coaches have been known to 'encourage' the rower by setting the resistance high and eating a bar of chocolate in front of the person training (as a joke).

Floor mats These are used for stretching to improve flexibility and for core stability exercises.

Music can help with training but your child needs to make sure that they set their MP3 player or iPod with suitable music, on the correct setting, as once they start a piece on the ergo, they cannot adjust it. There is nothing worse than listening to the same song for 20 minutes.

Water training

Boat clubs may have access to a river, a reservoir or a man-made lake. Man-made lakes have several advantages as they are less prone to flooding and are wider than natural rivers, allowing multi-lane racing. Their purpose-built side lanes enable the marshals to commentate on the events as they happen and spectators to have a better view. At the National Schools Regatta, for example, there are buses that allow spectators to see races as they progress along the entire course.

FACT *Special centres have been built to enable rowers to train and compete on multi-lane stretches of water. These are host to some of the major junior events. The first was the Holme Pierrepont in Nottingham, which opened in 1973. Dorney Lake near Eton opened in 2000 and the Redgrave Pinsent Rowing Lake opened in Caversham in 2006. This is where the GB rowing team trial and train.*

Before novices start rowing on any water, they must have passed a swim test and a capsize test. These tests are carried out under careful supervision and ensure that each rower knows what to do should they capsize whilst training or competing. The coaches have a duty of care to each member of their club which is taken very seriously, ensuring that rowers are sufficiently capable of taking to the water and know what to do should they encounter a difficulty. They follow the British Rowing guidelines which can be found on the British Rowing website at www.britishrowing.org.

Once they have completed their water tests, rowers will be taught about the equipment. They will soon learn the names of the different parts of the boats. These are included in the appendix section to give you an idea as well.

Boat clubs have very expensive equipment, which is housed in a very tight space. Boats and blades are stored on racks and each rower will be taught how to collect these without damaging them. They need to collect their blades first and place them by the water's edge before they collect their boat. The boats are usually stored rigged, so that rowers need to be careful not to damage the boat or surrounding boats with the riggers when they take them from the racks. They carry the boats by the gunwales and should never carry them by the riggers. The boats are stored upside down on the racks and are lifted off and usually carried above the heads of the rowers. There are drills to coordinate this procedure, usually called by the cox (or one rower in a coxless boat).

Each rower collects the boat that they will be rowing in, so that four people will carry a quad or four and eight people will carry an eight or octuple. Two people are needed to lift a single off the racks, but these can be carried by one person (with practise).

Once the boats are lifted, they are often placed directly onto the water (this is why they need their blades at the water's edge. If the boat is not rigged (before or after an event) or the rigging needs to be altered (for example from a quad to a four) it is placed on a trestle whilst the rigging is changed. The rowers need a rigger jigger (a special spanner) to be able to do this (more on this later).

Your son or daughter will learn how to place their boat on the water and how to get into it safely. There will be strict rules about all these things and the rowers will be expected to help others. There is a lot to learn at the start but they learn drills in order to make this safe. However, they do need to listen to the coaches and follow their instructions carefully.

Experienced crews make boating and rowing off from the water's edge look easy but one only needs to watch novice crews to know how complicated it can be when a rower is faffing around and holding the crew up.

When novices start to row they are often taken out on a training lead, until the coaches are satisfied that they are safe. Initially they will learn to scull with two blades, and later on to sweep using one. They most often row in quads when they first start as these boats are more stable than doubles or singles.

During a typical training session, rowers will row set distances up and down their stretch of water in different boats. During the winter months, the focus is on distance training and endurance (this could be the equivalent to 18k). In the summer they are more likely to practise short pieces for regattas.

'You might think that after training muscles for so long, repeating the same motion again and again, a crew race would be relatively easy – that the muscles would have their own memory and could simply take over while the mind sat back and went on automatic pilot ...'

DANIEL J. BOYNE, *THE RED ROSE CREW*, © LYONS PRESS, 2005

The crews are often mixed around. This can make the better rowers work harder (as they have to pull more to move the boat) and it gives the less experienced rowers the feeling of what it is like to row at a higher level. It is helpful to remind the older rower how lovely it was to be put with senior rowers when they were younger if they start to complain.

Some training sessions will be devoted to the process of selecting boats for races, which is often more complicated than meets the eye. Leading up to an event, your rower may announce that they are going to have time trials or seat races at their next training session in order to gain a place in a particular boat (more on this later).

Instead of rowing at a training session, your child may be asked to cox, and sometimes they may sit in a launch with the coach. Watching others is a very useful way of learning.

At the end of the session they need to be able to get out of the boat safely, and to be able to lift it from the water without injury to themselves, others or to the equipment. They may be asked to de-rig their boat. They will need to return the boats and blades to the correct places before they finish their session. This takes an extra 20 minutes or so after they leave the water (and longer if they faff around or chat).

Training schedules

FACT *The GB team train for three sessions a day. Typically they might spend 100 minutes on the water, in single sculls in the winter and in their crew boats in the summer seasons. At the second session they might do a 24k ergo and at the third, 100 minutes of strength and core stability work.*
INFORMATION FROM: WWW.INSPIREDBYROWING.ORG.UK

Training will vary depending on the season and your child's age and ability. In the winter, there is more endurance training. This takes the form of a run, often over 5 km, with varying intensities, or a gym-based session. Gym-based sessions are particularly held on weekdays, as it is dark in the evenings after school or college. Some rowers are lucky and can train at weekends during the winter on protected water. However, many find that their stretch of river can become flooded or at best restricted, in which case there is more land training.

Once the clocks change for the summer, the evenings are longer and water sessions after school are usually possible. Weekend sessions usually stay the same, although they can start earlier (e.g. 6 am leading up to an event).

EXAMPLE OF A TRAINING SCHEDULE

Year	Monday	Tuesday	Wednesday	Thursday	Friday	Saturday	Sunday
Novices	circuits ergo 4–6 pm				ergo run 4–6 pm	row water 8–10 am or 10–12 pm	
J13	circuits		circuits ergo 4–6 pm or row water 4–6 pm		ergo circuits 4–6 pm	row water 8–12 pm	row water 8–12 pm
J14	row water 4–6 pm		circuits ergo 4–6 pm	ergo circuits 4–6 pm		row water 8–12 pm	row water 8–12 pm
J15	weights circuits 4–6 pm	ergo run 4–6 pm	row water 4–6 pm	row water 4–6 pm		row water 8–12 pm	row water 8–12 pm
J16 and seniors	ergo weights 4–6 pm	row water 4–6.30 pm	ergo weights 4–6 pm	row water 4–6 pm		row water 8–12 pm	row water 8–12 pm

SAFETY

M ost clubs and schools will row on designated stretches of water, so that it is likely that the main safety issues relate to the weather.

Weather conditions

Rain, fog and wind may affect the water conditions and make it unsafe to row. Although training or an event may be in the diary, you may not know until the morning where your rower is going to be. This can be frustrating, particularly if you have other family commitments. Each club will run it's own system to alert you to any change to the rowing schedule.

There are three types of flags:

- green flag – all crews can row
- amber/grey flag – water conditions will be assessed by a senior coach and a decision made about whether or not a crew can row. Sometimes crews can go out in larger boats (octs or eights).
- red flag – novices and juniors cannot row. Senior crews may be able to row depending on the severity of the conditions.

FACT *The first modern Olympic Games were held in 1896 in Athens. Rowing was scheduled to take place in these Games but the regatta was called off owing to high seas. Rowing first took place at the next Games, held in Paris in 1900. The Olympic Games were due to be held in Rome in 1908, but the venue was changed to London when Mount Vesuvius erupted in 1906 (there was a sudden need to divert funds to those affected by the natural disaster).*
INFORMATION FROM: WWW.OLYMPICS.ORG.UK

It is important to understand that all coaches will follow the British Rowing guidelines. In November 2008 they updated their water safety code and replaced it with 'Row safe: A Guide to Good Practice in Rowing'.

What happens to training if rowing on the water is unsafe?

If this happens before training starts there are several possibilities:

- the rowers may be sent for a run – so they must have their running trainers with them at all river sessions
- they may be asked to do an indoor training session
- the session may be cancelled.

If the weather changes during a rowing session rowers may finish early. A mobile phone (turned on) is useful in these situations. Make sure your child has all the contact numbers on their phone (and that you do the same).

What happens at an event if weather conditions change?

Sadly, even in the summer months the weather can make conditions unsafe to compete. Adverse weather conditions may exist from the start of the day or develop during the day of an event. In these situations the Safety Advisor and Chairman of the Race Committee for the event will follow the safety guidelines from the British Rowing: 'Row safe: A Guide to Good Practice in Rowing'. and may decide to

- suspend the start of the race or event
- have a free start to the race rather than have the crews try to attach to a stake boat (more later)
- shorten the course
- change or limit the lanes used at regattas
- cancel the event.

It can be very disappointing for all involved (particularly if they have been building up to an event for weeks, and have had a very early start to the day).

> **FACT** *The National Schools Regatta has only been cancelled twice since it was first held in 1947. In 1987 the whole event was cancelled and in 2008 the rowing was stopped on the second day owing to the extreme weather conditions.* INFORMATION FROM: WWW.NSR.ORG.UK

Personal safety

It is important for rowers to take responsibility for their own safety at all times. This includes getting to and from rowing in the early hours or at night when it may be dark. Many rowers use bicycles to get to and from sessions. They should be careful if cycling alone, make sure that they are easily visible and carrying a mobile phone.

Once they start rowing, if the visibility is not good (but it is safe to row), a fluorescent jacket or top is helpful. If they are in a single, and out of site of the coaches, they need to be extra careful.

TIME OFF SCHOOL

It can be hard when your child starts rowing at the age of 11 to imagine how they will turn out at the age of 18. Many parents worry that rowing will negatively impact on examination results, with the concern that too many hours on the water means too few spent studying. Infact, in many cases the rowing has a positive affect on the student. This is because they have to be extremely organised with their studies and be prepared to catch up on any work missed.

The majority of rowing events take place at weekends; however, a few are held during the week. Your rower may need to take time off school to train just before an event or may need to travel during school hours to get to some of the major competitions. Your club will be able to tell you if and when your child will be asked to row in events that necessitate time off school. We detail some of the main events on page 69.

> **FACT** *Most rowers achieve stunning exam results and this has been well documented in the press. Perhaps less well known is the fact that many top rowers also excel at music, which is understandable as both skills require a good sense of rhythm.*

GB ROWING

The Junior GB selection process takes place over many months and only a few gain places in boats; however, it is a wonderful experience for those lucky enough to be invited to trial. By the time rowers are taking part in GB selection, they are juggling their rowing commitment with revision for GCSE, AS and A levels. FISA, the International Rowing Federation, has education as one of its core values. They recognise that rowing 'teaches self discipline and motivation together with committment and a spirit of fair play'.

> **FACT** *Pierre De Coubertin, who restarted the modern Olympics in 1896, was a rower. Men's rowing first took place at the Olympics in Paris in 1900. Women were first allowed to row in the Montreal Games in 1976 (albeit in one race).* INFORMATION FROM: WWW.OLYMPICS.ORG.UK

The first entry criterion for GB selection is a timed ergo piece in October. This is 2k at rate 24 with a cut off for boys of 7.05 minutes for J16 and 6.55 for J18. For girls it is sub 7.55 for WJ16 and 7.50 minutes for WJ18.

The few who achieve this go to trials in Boston, Lincolnshire, in November and February. For the February long-distance trials, they do a timed 5k ergo. Here, there is no discrimination between the age groups and the cut-off time on the ergo for boys is 17.50 minutes and for girls it is 20.10 minutes at rate 26. The rowers also do trials in singles. Some rowers then go on to do Spring Assessments in April, where the selection is made for the Munich Regatta. The 2k cut-off time on the ergo is 6.35 minutes for boys and 7.30 minutes for girls.

After this a few get invited to go to final trials. This leads to the teams for the World Rowing Junior Championships and also the Coupe de la Jeunesse. Final trials are normally held in June and July.

The times quoted were appropriate for the 2008/2009 season. They can change on a yearly basis by small amounts. The times are set when the GB coaches meet up for what they call their 'wash up' meeting in September.

There is also an opportunity for clubs to put together their own crews to trial for the J16 GB v France match. The selection process is different from the other GB trials, as school and club crews trial rather than individual rowers. Trials are held on one day at the end of June at Holme Pierrepont, Nottingham, and the selected crews go on to represent their country in July. The match is held either in France or Great Britain.

'Rowing for GB has been a dream. It's so exciting being in the team... The water was flying about and there were big waves hitting us, but we sneaked in front and then held them off at the finish. I hope I can make the GB team again at Coupe or Junior World level, as it's an amazing experience.' AN U16 GB ROWER (ROWING AND REGATTA MAGAZINE, AUGUST 2009)

The National Championships are also held at the beginning of July at Holme Pierrepont, Nottingham, and from here rowers who win events can trial for the Home Countries International Regatta. This takes place towards the end of July between England, Ireland, Scotland and Wales.

Selection for the Australian Youth Olympic Festival is every second year and is trialled separately from the above - you may have heard people refer to this as the 'Youth Olympics'. This started in 2000 following the Australian Olympic Games and gives young rowers the opportunity to train and race internationally using the Sydney Olympics facilities. Rowers are selected for U18 and U23 races, which are held in January (Australian summertime).

The Australian Youth Olympic Festival is different from the Youth Olympic Games. These new Olympic Games are open to 14–18 year olds. Rowing is part of the Summer Olympics and selections for boats take place following the results of the World Rowing Junior Championships.

The Commonwealth Rowing Championships are also every four years. Again this is separate from the main Commonwealth Games. There are no junior crews at this event.

'If anyone here is secretly dreaming of making the Olympics, I can tell you exactly how to do that in two words: Sustained Obsession. The obsession isn't so hard. But keeping it sustained is a tough nut to crack. A heartfelt enemy can go a long way to sustaining your obsession. Love your enemy.' BRAD ALAN LEWIS, *WANTED: ROWING COACH*, SHARK PRESS, 2007

HEALTH

O nce your rower becomes addicted to the sport, it can be difficult to pursuade them that for health reasons they should miss a training session. We have found the following advice helpful.

Can rowers train if they are unwell or injured?

You need to check with the coach if your child is unwell. If they have viral type symptoms but are well enough to survive school, it does not mean that they are safe to train or compete.

The pulse rate will normally rise at the start of an illness. Your rower may be advised to take his or her morning pulse to establish their 'normal' rate. This should be at rest. They only need to do this a few times. When he or she starts to feel unwell, they should re-take their pulse. If it is 20% above their normal rate, they should consider missing training and get advice from their coach. If a rower is ill they should stay away and not pass on germs. This is particularly important before big events when the crews need to remain healthy (it is why they are asked not to share water bottles).

If your child is injured, the coaches will advise accordingly. Do not wait for the injury to 'heal itself'. Seek advice from your GP – it is worth getting advice early as referrals to specialists can take time. The coaches should have details of sports physiotherapists with a local practice.

It is definitely not advisable to row through an injury. However, your rower may still be able to do some sort of training to keep their fitness up (e.g. swimming and cycling). The coaches can advise on this. They may also be able to sit in the launch at the river, which allows them valuable time with the coaches and they can learn from watching others.

It can be very dispiriting to be injured, so spending time with the coach and peer group helps. It can also take its toll on you. Do not be tempted to encourage your rower to row if they are not fit as they are unlikely to be able to perform at their best, which will be devastating, and it may prolong the injury or do serious harm.

Illness or injury during an event

Occasionally a rower or cox becomes ill or is injured on the day of an event. British Rowing has rules on what should happen in this situation. If it occurs before the first race of an event then it may be possible to make changes to the crew and if not, the boat may be scrapped. If it happens after racing has started, the rower or cox will need to be seen by the race officials. If they are deemed medically unfit, they can be replaced by another British Rowing registered rower from the same club, or any cox (the cox can be from a different club). Obviously this can be devastating for the rower or the cox and unsettling and upsetting for all concerned.

Heatstroke and sun exposure

It is very important for your child to protect him or herself against the effects of the sun. A hat, sunscreen, sunglasses and enough to drink are essential. Rowers are vulnerable because of the reflection of the UV rays off the water and they should be particularly careful to prevent sunburn and damage to their eyes. In the heat, they will sweat more and can rapidly become dehydrated, so they need to drink plenty of fluids. (For more information, see the section on this on page 43.) This applies to coxes as well as to the rowers.

Hypothermia

Conversely, rowing during the winter can be very demanding and without realising it your child can be at risk from hypothermia (when the body can no longer maintain its core temperature). In order to counteract this, it is important that they wear a hat and many layers of clothing. Multiple layers are more effective than one single layer. The outside layer should be wind and waterproof. They should wrap up and have a warm drink and snack immediately after training. If they become wet they should change out of these clothes as soon as possible. Coxes should wear additional layers as they are more at risk.

Boat bites and blisters

From now on your rower's hands and shins will never look the same. They will get blisters on their hands from the handles of the blades, and may catch their shins on the runners of the boat, causing 'boat bites'. Both of these can look dramatic at times with boat bites bleeding heavily (it often looks worse than it is and can be quite frightening to a novice rower). Some people recommend bathing these in salty water. Often hands and shins become hardened with time. If a large blister forms on the hands, it can be lanced with a sterile needle and cleaned. Large calluses can be filed. It is worth keeping on eye on any skin lesions to ensure that they do not become infected and it is a good idea to cover them during training sessions. Coaches may prefer that rowers use zinc oxide tape rather than elastoplasts or micropore tape as the latter stick to the equipment.

Existing medical conditions

Coaches need to be made aware of any existing medical conditions. These include asthma, diabetes, epilepsy, migraine and any severe allergy. Rowers need to make sure that they have their medications with them and also that the coaches know what to do and who to contact in an emergency.

Prevention of disease from the water

It is extremely important that rowers get into good habits to prevent contracting water borne infections, such as Weil's disease. They should:

- wash their hands before eating and ideally drinking
- make sure that mouthpieces of water bottles do not come into contact with the water
- keep cuts and blisters clean at all times
- keep their feet protected when launching a boat directly into the water. It is very tempting to walk around in bare feet but at larger events you will see experienced rowers have wellies on, which they throw to the shore or to a designated welly catcher!

Training during growth

During his or her adolescent years, your child will be growing rapidly and at different times from others. Some reach adult height more quickly; others are later to develop.

It is important not to over train during periods of rapid growth. This means that coaches may monitor their athletes' height and weight at regular intervals.

Arm lengths and sometimes leg measurements are recorded to ensure that rowers are each given the correct rig for their seat in the boat (this is rather like setting up a bike). They may need to adjust the seat position and footplate settings as they grow. Some rowers sit on a special raised 'boat seat'. This is used either for comfort, or to help with the basic rigging of the boat for the individual. Rowers who have long shins will have knees that sit higher in the boat so it is difficult to reach over them at the beginning of the stroke (drive 1 on the stroke cycle – see page 50). Raising the level of the pelvis by using a boat seat makes this manoeuvre easier.

Developing and maintaining flexibility is important especially during growth spurts and your rower should warm up and down after sessions to protect their muscles.

Hamstring muscles in particular can quickly become very tight and this may reduce a rower's performance as well as putting strain on the lower back. This is because rowers need to be able to tilt their pelvis to reach over during the recovery phase of the stroke cycle (see position in 'recovery 3'). If a rower has tight hamstrings then they will not be able to tilt their pelvis at the correct angle in order to do this and will over use their lumbar and thoracic spine instead. This can cause pain in the back muscles or more serious injury.

If your rower starts to complain that their back is hurting after a session, talk to their coach. It may be that they need to work on their hamstring muscles. Stretching and flexibility exercises are good for rowers and parents alike and can be done anywhere in the world (even, with a little encouragement, whilst watching the television).

At all times maintaining core stability is vital, particularly to prevent back injuries. This advice applies to rowers of all abilities and aspirations. We provide an example of core stability exercises in the appendix section.

Secret diary of a rowing slave

TIME sometime before 6 am

DATE Sunday 9 January

SETTING kitchen at home – work surfaces cluttered with evidence of previous night's excesses

HAIR wild

CAFFEINE STATUS zero. Looking for coffee beans. Tempted to re-use old grains.

In kitchen, in pyjamas. Realise that need carb-loading pasta meal for race. Really must learn to do all this the night before. Find supermarket pasta sauce and pour over pasta in vague attempt to look appetizing. Present pasta to offspring with smug flourish. Response of children derails reputation as Domestic Goddess. Pasta is still uncooked.

Pasta status corrected, stomach sinks again — remember rash promise to make chocolate brownies for crew at regatta. Amazingly find chocolate sponges in leftover Tupperware from the last week's birthday tea. Bash them about a bit with rolling pin and douse with icing sugar — have achieved task — it's official, am now a 'Rowing Super Mum'.

That only leaves breakfast, packing the car and transforming self into presentable parent — must remember to change out of PJs and slippers this time or will be disowned once more.

Ready to leave feel as if have just run an army assault course and it's only 6.30 am. Close the house door … and hear snoring noises from upstairs … must be bliss … what is a lie in?

NUTRITION

Nutrition is the science of what the body needs to eat and drink in relation to its requirements and physiology. The body can only perform to its full potential if the athlete is aware of what he or she needs to eat and drink. It is like making sure that there is enough petrol in a car so that it does not break down.

'Breakfast can be toast, cereal or porridge, and we can order anything cooked from the chef. We have a dietary target of 6000 calories a day, and though it sounds as though you can eat anything you like, you must try to get 70% of that total in carbohydrate.' INFORMATION FROM:

A LIFETIME IN A RACE MATTHEW PINSENT © EBURY PRESS

It is surprisingly difficult to get good information about what a young rower should eat, written in one place, and advice that is easily transferable into school and family life. We hope that the following information is helpful. It has been written with the school rower in mind. By this we mean rowers who are training and racing regularly with their club or school at junior level.

Having said that, it is worth noting that an 11-year-old novice rower will have different nutritional requirements when compared to those of a full-grown 18 year old athlete in the first eight. We have tried to give guidance on these differences. The needs of boys and girls will also vary as they grow. Planning a growing rower's nutritional requirements is therefore a continuous process that you will need to review regularly.

rower becomes more senior, and his or her training and racing
demands increase, you may wish to seek further advice from the coach or from
a qualified sports nutritionist. Similarly, if your rower has a special dietary need
we would also advise that you seek a specialist opinion.

What do rowers need to eat and drink on a day-to-day basis?

A well-balanced diet should be sufficient for most novice rowers who are not
training regularly or at high intensity. Once they increase their exercise they
need to look at their nutrition in more detail and they need to be aware that
their dietary requirements will be greater than their non-rowing friends. They
may need to eat more than those friends, should not skip meals and should
choose carefully from school menus.

As with all diets, it is important for them to eat from the main nutrient groups
which are:

- carbohydrates
- protein
- minerals and vitamins
- fats
- fluids.

Carbohydrates

Carbohydrates provide the main source of energy during exercise. The body
stores small amounts of carbohydrate in the liver and muscles and this is known
as glycogen. Glycogen is broken down more easily than fat, which is the body's
other source of energy, and is therefore essential during physical activity.
Because the body only stores small amounts of glycogen, this is used up
quickly. If it is not replenished by consuming sufficient carbohydrates, the
athlete's performance will become sluggish and they will fatigue more quickly.

In order to build up stores of glycogen it is recommended that an athlete should consume 60% of his or her diet as carbohydrates. For a younger athlete or novice rower this can be nearer to 50%, which is the normal amount of carbohydrate in a 'British' diet.

A good guideline to use is for your rower to consume 7–10g of carbohydrate per kg of body mass. An easy way to remember this is that your rower's plate of food should be two thirds carbohydrate, as a rough visual guide.

Protein

Protein plays a major part in repair and recovery after exercise. It additionally helps the immune system and hormone production. Every living animal and plant cell has protein as one of its main constituents. Protein is made up of amino acids, and we need to eat foods containing amino acids as our bodies are unable to create them from scratch. Amino acids from our diet are then used to form new proteins, which have many uses in our bodies, for example in muscles and as part of haemoglobin in the blood.

An athlete should consume between 1.2 and 1.4g of protein per kg of body weight per day. This is about 10–15% of the total calories and this is much lower than you might expect.

Most rowers will find that they already eat enough protein if they have a diet containing meat, fish, eggs and dairy products. Pulses, seeds and nuts are also sources of protein but these do not contain all the amino acids they need, so vegetarians should be careful to get their protein from a range of sources. They may need to get additional dietary advice on this.

Excess amino acids from the diet do not get turned into spare muscle, so there is no benefit in having a high protein diet or taking amino acid supplements as these alone will not make your rower have more muscle. British Rowing has strict guidance on supplements and this can be found on their website.

Minerals and vitamins

Iron is particularly important for athletes owing to the breakdown of muscle during exercise. Iron is also needed for the production of haemoglobin in the blood, and part of its function is to carry oxygen and nutrients to muscles and waste products away.

Vegans need to be particularly careful to have a high iron content diet because they are not getting iron from other sources, such as meat, fish and dairy products. Vegetarians can get iron from green leaf vegetables, pulses, dried fruit, fortified breakfast cereals and bread. However, red meat contains the most iron.

It is also worth noting that the absorption of iron from the diet is poor, and can be improved by taking iron with vitamin C (ascorbic acid). An easy way to do this is for rowers to drink fresh orange juice when they eat their breakfast cereals or toast.

Equally importantly, certain substances (phytates and oxolates) in food prevent the absorption of iron from the diet. These are found in tea, soya protein, rhubarb and spinach. So these are best consumed at a different time.

If your rower starts to feel tired or has repeated colds, then it may be worth checking that they are not deficient in iron. This can be checked by a blood test.

Calcium is important for any growing teenager. Calcium is needed to form bones and also helps the function of skeletal muscles and the heart. Dairy products such as milk and cheese and low fat yoghurts are good sources of calcium and smaller amounts are present in bread. Skimmed milk contains more calcium than full fat milk. Other non-dairy sources are bony fish (sardines where the small bones are eaten) and vegetables such as broccoli and cabbage. Like iron, some substances reduce the absorption of calcium from the diet: cocoa, soya beans, spinach, wheat bran and wholemeal cereals.

It does not seem necessary to take additional vitamin or mineral supplements if your son's or daughter's diet contains enough iron and calcium. This is because foods that are high in these also contain enough of the other elements.

Fats

Your natural instinct may be that a low fat diet is best for your family. However, fat is an important part of the diet for many reasons – including brain function, eye function, the immune system and temperature regulation, all important for rowers. The recommended amount of fat intake is less than 25% of total calories.

Nevertheless, it is the type of fat that is important. The diet should be rich in monounsaturated and polyunsaturated fats rather than saturated fats. Unfortunately, it is the saturated fats that are contained in most of the delicious food that our children like to eat, i.e. cakes and biscuits. The 'good' fats can be found in oily fish, leafy green vegetables, nuts and seeds (which are less tempting).

Fluids

It is important to drink enough fluids and it is generally thought that this should be about 2 litres a day. With exercise this will be more. Some clubs weigh their top rowers before and after training sessions to see how many kilograms they have lost during the session. For each kilogram lost a rower needs to drink 1.5 litres of fluid.

Your child should be encouraged to take a water bottle to school to ensure that he or she can drink freely during the day. By the time they are feeling thirsty, the chances are they are already dehydrated. You can also tell them that the colour of their urine is a good indicator. If it is yellow or dark yellow, they need to drink more. They will also find that they are better able to concentrate and focus if they are well hydrated and drinking enough during the day.

This advice applies to coxes and parents as well as rowers (particularly on event days when you are busy rushing around and have had a very early start and so are out of your normal routine).

Dental care

Sports drinks, particularly the fizzy ones, damage the enamel of teeth, owing to their high sugar and acid content. The best method of avoiding tooth decay is to drink via a straw and to avoid swilling the liquid around the mouth. Ideally your child should rinse their mouth with water after drinking these. Obviously this is not always possible but being aware of the potential problem helps. You should talk to a dentist if you are worried.

Meal planning

Rowers should have three meals a day. Breakfast is particularly important and rowers may need to eat more than they would normally choose to at that time of day. Even if the family is running late, try not to skip breakfast and allow enough time for this in your busy schedule.

In the appendix we have included a rower's meal guide to help them make their choices at school lunchtime. It gives an indication of what can and should be eaten during the day for maximum performance, both in the classroom and on the water.

What should rowers eat and drink prior to training?

In addition to a well-balanced diet, most rowers will be encouraged to take some form of snack and a drink before training. As much of this training goes on after school, rowers may need to pack a snack and drink in the morning to take with them to school. It can be difficult for parents to know which snacks are nutritious, easily portable in school bags and likely to be consumed.

Some easy snacks are:

- banana, kiwi and dried fruit
- low fat yoghurt or fromage frais
- cereal bars

- oat cakes
- malt loaf
- bagels
- scones
- crackers
- fruit smoothie.

The timing of the snack is also important. Ideally it should be eaten 1–2 hours before exercise (for reasons we explain in the next section on racing diets). However, this is not normally possible and the above snacks can be easily consumed in the car or minibus on the way to rowing. Most of these will keep in a rowing bag without needing to be refrigerated.

They should also arrive at rowing adequately hydrated, and they should drink 300–400 mls of water (or 5 mls per kg of body weight) at least 30 minutes before they start so, again, on the way to rowing.

What should rowers eat and drink during training?

The amount of food and fluid needed to replace losses during exercise will vary depending on the length and intensity of the exercise and the weather conditions. In higher temperatures the body will sweat more and fluids and electrolytes will need to be replaced at a greater rate. During long pieces or pieces of high intensity, glycogen will be broken down and this will need to be replaced by carbohydrates, either in fluid or snack form. This is in addition to replacing water and electrolytes.

Essentially there are three types of fluid replacement; they differ in the amount of electrolytes and carbohydrates that they replenish. The types are:

- hypotonic drinks
- isotonic drinks
- hypertonic drinks.

Hypotonic drinks

Hypotonic drinks consist of water with electrolytes and very low levels of carbohydrate. They are used when the athlete is concerned about rapid fluid replacement without the need to boost energy levels. So they are useful for novices and lighter training sessions. If hypotonic drinks are used for heavier training sessions alone, the rower will quench their thirst but will not replace loss in the cells, so they will fatigue more easily. They should use isotonic solutions in these situations. Examples of hypotonic drinks are low-calorie drinks and very diluted squash.

Isotonic drinks

Isotonic drinks are electrolyte drinks with 6-8% levels of carbohydrate. They have the same electrolyte balance as plasma in the blood and help hydrate the cells of tissues, unlike the hypotonic solutions. This is a very simplified explanation, as the science is quite complex. These drinks replace electrolyte and energy loss and are the best to aid rehydration during heavier training sessions and in the heat. Isotonic drinks can be found in supermarkets or ordered online. They can come in powder form and can be made up with water just before the session.

Hypertonic drinks

Hypertonic drinks are electrolyte drinks, with some protein and high levels of carbohydrate. They are useful during the recovery phase mainly, although they can also be used after long pieces in training when carbohydrate refuelling is necessary. The small amounts of protein they contain aid the storage of glycogen during recovery. These drinks are more usually found in specialist sports shops and can also be ordered online. They are also available in powder form and some are labelled as recovery drinks.

Owing to the large number of marketed energy drinks, it can be difficult to know what rowers should consume and when. They can also be very expensive. With all these drinks it is vital that rowers follow the instructions on the labelling and understand which type of drink they are consuming.

Our understanding is that:

- for low to moderate intensity training sessions or sessions of less than an hour and in normal weather conditions, **water** should be sufficient; for most novices, this is all that they will need
- for moderate to high intensity training sessions or those lasting over an hour or in warm weather use the **isotonic** drinks
- for very long pieces at high intensity during training or for recovery after racing when higher level carbohydrate as well as electrolyte refuelling is necessary, then **hypertonic** drinks are appropriate.

Coaches will be able to advise you on whether this is needed.

Snacks

Snacks are another way of replacing carbohydrates and they help to prevent the rower from feeling tired during a long session, as well as being needed in the recovery phase. Most sessions will include a timed snack break. Suitable snacks are the same as the ones for pre session, but in practice the following are easy to leave near the water:

- cereal bars
- dried fruit
- rice cakes with jam
- malt loaf
- fruit gums.

How does this advice differ when racing?

The week before

You may have heard the term carbohydrate loading. For the important events in the rowing calendar, the crews in the senior boats may be asked to eat specific diets for the week before the event and have a specially tailored training regime, typically resting the day before. Our experience is that this only happens when your rower reaches a top crew.

Carbohydrate loading is thought to increase the endurance of rowers and improve performance by increasing the glycogen stores in the muscles. This enables rowers to row for longer without tiring (which is important when they are rowing for the finish line against rival crews).

This diet generally has even higher carbohydrate content than the usual training diet although rowers don't need to eat more in total. Whilst eating a very high carbohydrate diet, they will need to drink more fluids and also avoid fluids that contain caffeine (such as coffee, tea and coke drinks) as these can be dehydrating. Coaches will give advice on this.

On the day of the race

Rowers need to start the day with a good breakfast and this may need to be very early in the morning, 3–4 hours before they are due to race. They can then have a snack 2–3 hours before the race as they are advised not to eat within 1–2 hours of racing. They can, however, drink hypotonic and isotonic fluids during this time.

Our understanding is that if the rower eats too close to a race, their performance may be hampered. This is because not only may it be uncomfortable, as the food sits in the digestive tract, but it also interferes with the release of energy during exercise. This is because insulin is produced about 20 minutes after eating. Insulin regulates the blood sugar level, and one of its functions is to prevent fats from being released from cells, and so stored glycogen is broken down instead. The body only has small reserves of glycogen. Essentially this means that at the time when the rower needs the most energy in the race, they will have the least reserve.

As the insulin response is not immediate, the rower can eat a high-energy snack 5–10 minutes before they race, such as jelly beans or fruit gums. This will give a short energy boost when they need it (unless the start is delayed).

What should rowers eat and drink after training and racing?

The first two hours after exercise are essential for replacing glycogen stores. This is called the recovery phase – an athlete should aim to consume 1g of carbohydrate per kilogram of body weight during the first two hours following exercise. The sooner the carbohydrate is consumed the better (within 30 minutes is ideal) as glycogen is restored nearly one and a half times more quickly than normal during this time.

After training this is easy to organise as the rowers can have their snack once they are off the water or on the way home. In our experience, rowers often forget to eat soon after an event for a number of reasons:

- it may take a while for them to come off the water (especially when they need to wait to be marshalled back to the boating area)
- they may have their food and drink in their kit bags a distance away from the end of a race
- they may need to have a team talk
- they may be feeling so tired that they feel sick and don't feel like eating or drinking
- they may be celebrating their successes!
- they may be trying to ignore advice from their parents as it is considered to be 'fussing'.

So refuelling becomes delayed. However, the good news is that rowers can eat chocolate within their replacement, which is easy to have ready at the end of the race and can be washed down with fluids. In this way they can start their refuelling at the time that most counts.

Your rower will know his or her own weight in kilograms. An easy way to calculate a rower's needs is to approximate snacks in terms of 50g units (for each 50 kilograms of body weight). For example, 50g of carbohydrate can be found in a 75g Mars bar or a 100g Snickers bar, but your son or daughter would need to eat eight fingers of Kit Kat.

However, it is more sensible for your son or daughter to get their carbohydrate and protein replacement from varied sources. These include:

- a wholemeal sandwich with chicken or tuna filing
- pasta with vegetable sauce
- baked beans on toast
- two cereal bars.

We have added a list of snacks that give 50g of carbohydrate in our appendix as a useful guide (you can adjust this for your son or daughter according to their weight). They also need to remember to replace their fluid loss.

QUESTIONS ABOUT ROWING

Your child will soon find it embarrassing if you start talking about rowing, as clearly in their eyes you will not know very much! The following are questions that we needed to ask to find out more about this incredible sport.

What is the stroke cycle?

The stroke cycle is a series of movements in a continual motion which the rower uses to move the blades through the water. Rowers generally learn to scull first with two blades and then adapt this action when they start to sweep with one blade. For sculling, the blades enter the water at drive1 on the stroke cycle diagram (also called the catch). The rower is at the front of the slide (frontstops) and legs are compressed and the body and arms are stretched forwards. Over the next four phases (drive 2–5), the power of the stroke comes from the leg movement, the legs press down and the back and arms move backwards, and the seat moves towards the bow (backstop position drive 5 on the diagram). To a non-rower it might seem as if the strength comes from the upper body, but it should be driven from the legs (this takes a while to learn). The blades leave the water when the rower presses down on the handles of the blades at recovery 1 on the diagram. The next three movements (recovery 2–4) take the rower back to the catch, so that the arms lengthen again, the body rocks forward and the legs bend. The rowers should not rush this movement. Experienced rowers make this look smooth and effortless, they take their time and it is beautiful to watch.

Your child will practise this on an ergo machine until it becomes second nature. They should be able to explain it to you in more detail or to demonstrate it to you on an ergo machine.

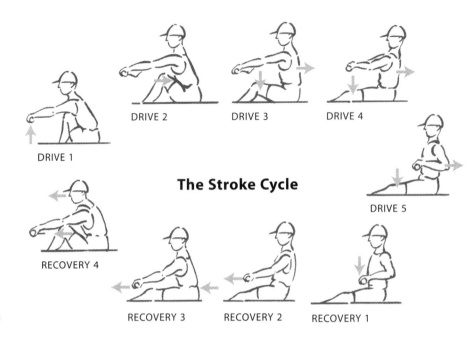

DRIVE 2   DRIVE 3   DRIVE 4

DRIVE 1

The Stroke Cycle

DRIVE 5

RECOVERY 4

RECOVERY 3   RECOVERY 2   RECOVERY 1

POWER (DRIVE) PHASE

Drive 1: The rower is at the front of the slide. Shins are vertical. Lower back is in a strong position.

Drive 2: The start of the drive. The initial drive is taken with legs only. Lower back is held firm.

Drive 3: Leg drive continues. Pressure being felt in the fingers. No lift in the shoulders.

Drive 4: Knees are being pressed down. Shoulders squeezed back.

Drive 5: Lower back is held strong and tall at the finish. As the arms complete the draw forearms should come through horizontally, without letting the elbows drop down.

RECOVERY PHASE

Recovery 1: Blade is tapped out of the water at the finish. On to the thighs. The trunk is held firm in the finish position.

Recovery 2: Hands are moving away from the body. Knees remain down until the elbows go over the knees.

Recovery 3: Body rocks over from the hips onto the knees in a strong position.

Recovery 4: The knees break and the weight bears down on the feet. The rower slowly moves up the slide ready to take another stroke.

Why record ergo times?

Ergo machines are an essential tool for the improvement of your child's rowing, but they are not always viewed with affection! They can be set at different levels of resistance, making it easier or harder to push (pushing with legs rather than pulling with arms).

Coaches will keep a record of rowers' ergo times in order to continuously monitor their progress and as part of selection for boats. At the start of the season it can take a while to get back to top form.

Sometimes your child may train with a covered screen, which helps them to work at an optimal level without the distraction of numbers. This suits some rowers better and helps when they are back on the water setting their own pace.

Rowers may talk about doing 'pieces' on the ergo, which can be either set distances e.g. 2 kilometres (2k) or certain lengths of time e.g. 15 minutes. They may tell you their 'split'. This is the average time to complete 500m. It will be in minutes and seconds and they might say their split was, for example, '2.05' for a certain piece. The lower the split, the more impressive! For some pieces, they may be asked to row at a set stroke rate, e.g. 24 and at other times the rate is 'free' so they can choose the rate that suits them.

Each rower will know their 'PB', or personal best for that piece. Seconds count and these matter hugely (the mood of your journey home can depend on how well your rower has done during a recorded piece on the ergo).

What does 'rigging' or 'de-rigging' the boat mean?

Setting the rigging of a boat is a complex process and usually done by the boatman or an experienced coach.

When boats are transported to and from events, the riggers and seats are normally removed before they are loaded on the trailer. This is called 'de-rigging'. The riggers are easily damaged and also need to be removed to ease the process of loading the boats onto the trailer. The footplates are attached to the boat and are not removed.

The shells of eights or octs are too long to fit on a trailer in one piece and these are dismantled into sections before they are loaded.

Both the seats and the riggers need to be replaced before boating, this is referred to as 'rigging'. The rowers learn to do this themselves, using their small spanners called rigger jiggers to tighten or loosen the bolts that attach the riggers to the shell. The shell of an oct or eight needs to be assembled, and the outriggers attached in either an eight or oct configuration. The seats slot onto the slides.

The positions of the footplates, the gate of the riggers, the position of the blades in the gates and the length of the movement of the seats along the slides can be altered to enable optimal racing. These are set up for each rower according to his or her height, arm length, flexibility, strength and expertise.

The riggings for a boat are set up so that all the rowers are in the same position on the slide at the end of the stroke. Variations in size and strength of individual crew members are accounted for by rigging in this way.

If the weather conditions change during an event, the settings of the rigging may be adjusted. In this situation the coaches may also tape the riggers. This means that they wrap a special boat tape around the riggers where they attached to the boat, forming a band, so that water from waves hits this tape and bounces back rather than going into the boat. This helps to keep water out of the boat.

What about coxing?

Coxes often start to row first and then switch to coxing. It helps if they feel part of the team and join in at land training sessions, although they do not need to achieve the same levels of fitness. Girls may find that they are coxing male crews as well as female ones when they become more experienced.

If a coach is directing your son or daughter towards coxing, see it as a positive thing – it may be because they see a good future for him or her in that area.

Coxes have been described as 'small, loud and bossy'; however, do not underestimate their importance. They do much more than just steer the boat. A good cox can win the race for the crew. They need to be able to:

- check that all the equipment is there and working
- work closely with the coaches and go through the race plan
- give out clear instructions
- work closely with the crew
- be able to understand the needs of the crew
- have the full attention and respect of the crew
- relax the crew before the race
- ensure that they boat on time, and in order, and that they are attached at the start and ready to race on time – this is more difficult than it seems in windy weather
- make the crew work together as a team
- get a good start to any race
- steer the boat through the course (avoiding all obstacles)
- read the wind and water conditions and make appropriate adjustments
- select the fastest lines for the race with minimal use of the rudder
- get a good finish
- ensure the safety of the boat and the rowers.

The cox uses a coxbox, which acts as a microphone so their instructions are heard by all members of the crew. It also gives the stroke rate, so the cox can change the rate of the crew accordingly, and the time of the race or session. Once a cox becomes more experienced at coxing he or she will also use a dictaphone, and record their races so that all their instructions to the rowers are stored on tape. These are analysed later by the coaches. At GB selection, the recordings are analysed and selections made on this basis.

There are two possible positions for a cox, stern or bow. So the cox is either behind the rowers or in front of them. Front loading boats are often faster.

Steering of any boat is vital and clearly having a cox can make a tremendous difference. Coxless boats are faster than coxed boats as they are lighter but they are more difficult to manoeuvre down a winding course. In a coxless boat, the rower at bow is given the task of steering the boat. They can do this either by using their blades and putting more or less pressure on one blade to move the boat, or by turning one of their feet, which is attached to a steering wire that controls the rudder. For any boat, each time the rudder is on, the boat slows down by approximately one foot per stroke, so rowers are encouraged to limit their use. It is better to make changes using the blades, which is what happens in a single scull.

Before a race, the crew or rower will need to make sure that they follow all the jobs of the cox, i.e. warming up, boating on time, getting to the start, attaching on to the stake boat etc. This proves that in a coxless boat the partnership between the crew is vital.

'The perception of a cox is someone who sits in a boat and doesn't do very much. Many people think that this is a relaxing job and looks a good place to get a suntan on a hot sunny day. In fact, coxing is much more complicated and is harder work than you think. I never thought that there would be so many different ways you could steer the boat, read a race plan, cross the river, rig a boat … the list goes on!!' EMMA BROWN W18 1ST EIGHT COX

FACT *The cox in the Oxford Cambridge Boat Race must have a minimum weight of 55kg. If the cox is underweight they must carry deadweight to make up the difference. In 1981 a woman coxed the Oxford crew for the first time and in 1985 a woman coxed for Cambridge. In 1989 both crews were coxed by women.* INFORMATION FROM: WWW.BOATRACE.ORG

What is a race plan?

When a cox is asked to make a race plan, they are planning the race not only from their point of view but also for the rowers. They need to be able to steer the course according to the circulation plan, know any bends or obstructions and be able to anticipate them. They should find out where the strong currents are, where they need to change bank and where the best passing places are. For some stretches of water they may use well-documented landmarks, such as the second lamp post on Hammersmith Bridge in the Schools' Head of the River race.

For the rowers, the race plan is a series of instructions on how to row the course. Each club varies, but on the whole a race plan is divided into 250m sections:

The start or first 250m
- first 3–5 strokes being short, sharp strokes
- next 5–10 strokes lengthen and build the rate
- some clubs will push gradually to get to maximum speed
- and some will go for a fast start and then come down to the race rate that they can sustain. This is normally a rate of 34–36 strokes and is called the 'stride'.

The second 250m is when the crew establish their race rhythm

The next 1000m is really about racing the race and getting ahead of the opposition – this is where skilled coxing makes all the difference; the crew will maintain their race rate with a series of pushes

In the last 250m they will pick up the speed of the boat and go for the finishing line!

'As a cox, you need to get to know what every facial expression for each crew member means and you can see when people are working well, and not so well!'

EMMA BROWN W18 1ST EIGHT COX

FACT *The course of the Schools' Head of the River race is 4.5 miles from Mortlake to Putney Bridge. There are four bends and two bridges to negotiate, and differences in the stream make the conditions unpredictable for the coxes. The Oxford and Cambridge Boat Race is the same course rowed in the opposite direction.*

What happens if the boat capsizes or sinks?

When a rower is a novice, he or she might expect to capsize from time to time, even in good weather conditions. However, it is possible that your child may capsize in any weather conditions at any stage in his or her rowing career. It is not uncommon for this to happen just after the finish line, particularly when a rower is in a single. This can be in their quest for the line or because they have exhausted themselves during the race and loose concentration once they are over the finish line.

If someone capsizes they must stay with their boat. This is for three reasons:

- the boat is a buoyancy aid
- to prevent hypothermia – they should lift themselves out of the water (as much as possible) onto the upturned boat
- to prevent injury – they may be injured or hit by another crew if they try to swim to the bank, particularly if it is in a head race or training where there are other crews approaching at speed who may not see them, as they are facing the wrong way. If it is very windy they may not hear well either.

At events there will be trained race marshals in lifeboats down the course who will rescue the rowers and take them to the finish of the race.

FACT *Rowers are most likely to capsize in a single scull. Crews are unlikely to capsize in an oct or eight, but they might sink. At the National Schools Regatta in 2008 several eights sank in extreme weather conditions. There have been six sinkings so far in the Oxford and Cambridge Boat Race, three of which determined the result of the race: Cambridge twice (in 1859 and 1978) and Oxford once (1925). The race can be rescheduled if a boat sinks before they have rowed to the end of the wall at the start of the race, if it is not due to a fault of a rower in the crew.* INFORMATION FROM: WWW.BOATRACE.ORG

As an observer, if you see a rower in the water and the race marshal has not arrived, you should phone your coach on his or her mobile. Warn other crews to move out when a rower is in the water in order to avoid a collision. Call for a race marshal, although they should already be on their way. You will need to take the rower's kit bag to the finish, so that they can shower, change into dry clothing and have a hot drink.

Very rarely, a boat may start sinking if it takes on too much water in very windy conditions and the same rules apply. The rowers will be aware that the boat is taking on water and if it occurs during a race, there will be race marshals in a rescue boat nearby to help them. They can usually stay in their boat until they are rescued as modern boats are designed to stay afloat. This is likely to be due to the weather conditions, with wind stirring up waves that go into the boat, rather than a fault with the boat itself. Taping the riggers can help in this situation as previously mentioned.

How does your child progress through the boat club?

It takes a long time to be able to row with good technique. Every season is different. Your rower may improve steadily over the seasons and years. Equally, he or she may have a fantastic season, and then the following season may go less well. It is very hard for rowers and parents alike.

There are many reasons for variations in performance. All children mature at different rates; they may have times when they are growing and tired; or they may have heavy academic commitments and find it hard to go that extra mile (literally). They may also have periods of injury or illness.

By mid teens they may be noticing other attractions outside of rowing, so become less focused. It is not uncommon to have periods of self doubt, when they find it hard to improve on their times or technique, and when they start to wonder if it is all worth it.

It can be more difficult for rowers to win at events as they get older. This is partly because some schools and clubs start rowing later, so there are fewer J12 entries than J16. So if your child has many medals as a novice it does not necessarily follow that they will have as many successes as a J18.

These are just some of the reasons why a rower may find that he or she is no longer in the boat they expected to be in. They should not assume that because they were in the first boat for an event that they will be in it for the next one. Parents should not assume this either. Places need to be earned for each race and performances can change for all the reasons listed above (and probably others that we have not thought of).

'In rowing, explaining the success of an underrated crew is almost as difficult as accounting for the poor performance of a highly favoured one'

DANIEL J. BOYNE, *THE RED ROSE CREW*, © LYONS PRESS, 2005

It is easy to read, and for us to write, these words. However, when this happens it can be all consuming. Rowing, as many sports, is extremely tough. However, often rowers will come out of this with great strength of character and skills that will last them for the rest of their life.

How do the coaches make their selections?

Selecting a crew for a boat is more complicated than it seems. Each coach will have their own criteria in order to make their selections and we have listed the ones that we know about! The first three are obvious but are included for the novice rower.

- safety – can the crew get from A to B without doing themselves harm?
- injury prevention – is their posture good enough to get them from A to B without doing themselves harm?
- technique – can they row together safely without causing injury?
- attendance – at some clubs and schools this is an important factor.

- water performance – scull ranking. Depending on the type of boat that a rower is trialling for, he or she will be assessed by looking at their seat racing results and/or pairs/doubles matrix and/or sculling ranking. If coaches are selecting a scull, scull ranking is vital. If they are selecting an eight, a pairs matrix is used. For a quad, it is a doubles matrix. Lastly, for a pair or double, a pairs or doubles matrix is used (more on this later).
- training performance – it is likely that the coach will have a record of all of a rower's ergo times, weight and strength tests, run times and swimming performances throughout the year.

'The composition of the crew was like the composition of a good photo; it had to have both balance and clarity. This required an excellent eye for detail, of knowing each rower's individual style and ability, in order to place them well in relation to the rest of the crew.' DANIEL J. BOYNE,

THE RED ROSE CREW, THE LYONS PRESS, 2005

Rowing camps

Many schools and clubs hold rowing camps, where final selections for the major events are made. The camps are generally held at a location away from the club, and may be abroad. Rowers train throughout the day on consecutive days, so coaching is very intensive. The camps are very enjoyable but exhausting. Rowers learn a great deal and the camps are a good chance for a crew to find out more about each other. The rowers need a great deal of kit for the camps and a large bin liner in which to collect dirty washing! In our experience, rowers often arrive home exhausted and need several days to rest before they unwind.

How should parents and coaches work together?

A good relationship between coaches and parents is vital. As a parent it is important to realise that, within each club, all coaches will have different rowing and coaching experiences. Some will have rowed for their country, others to a high club or school level. Some coaches may never have rowed themselves. Needless to say, all coaches will be Criminal Records Bureau (CRB) vetted.

Owing to the structure of coaching in many boat clubs, rowers may well have more than one coach. It is helpful to know which one you should go to with your questions. In most cases, it is appropriate to go to the designated coach for your child's year group, rather than straight to the top coach. There may be times in your child's rowing career when you feel surprised by the boat selections. Many coaches welcome all sorts of questions and would be happy to have a discussion about the reasons behind specific selections of boats if you are concerned. However, you should not challenge them on what they know best. It could only put your own blood pressure up and it will not change the selection of crews!

Good questions to ask the coaches could be:

- What can be done to improve my rower's chances of being in the top boat?
- How can we help with this?
- What can the coaches do to help? (Normally they will already be doing this, but it is worth asking).

A few golden rules are helpful:

- treat the coaches as you would like to be treated yourself
- lead by example – if you question the ability of the coaches in front of your son or daughter, they may follow your example
- support the coaches, especially when a discipline issue arises
- go to events and support both the coaches and the rowers.

But:

- do not shout at the coaches (it happens more than you could imagine)
- do not phone the coaches after working hours (it similarly happens more than you could ever imagine – especially after 9 pm on a Friday night).

The coaches give out their mobile numbers for emergency use only for events and on trips. So, before you phone or text out of hours, think:

- is this really a rowing emergency?
- would I be contacting any other member of the teaching staff about a problem at school or college?
- do I really need to be involved, or can my son or daughter sort this out?

'Not everybody wins, and certainly not everybody wins all the time. But once you get into your boat and push off, tied into your shoes and boot stretchers, then "lean on the oars", you have indeed won far more than those who have never tried.' ANON.

KIT

As with any sport your young rower will soon acquire a huge amount of kit, necessary for both training and competitions.

Why do rowers need such large bags?

For training sessions, rowers need to take many more things with them than you might imagine, in order to cover all possible outcomes (rain, wind, capsizing, blisters, more rain … and even some sun).

Trainers Rowers will need a good pair of these. This is to help to prevent injury to ankles, knees and hips. It is recommended that you go to a specialist shop to have trainers fitted. Although this is expensive, the cost of the trainers will be less than the cost of a course of osteopathy or physiotherapy treatments. Rowers need to have their trainers with them at all sessions. Trainers that have been for a swim in the river or become wet on runs soon smell. So encourage your rower to rinse and dry them as soon as possible! (They usually forget and you then discover them when there is a dreadful smell exuding from their kit bag).

Clothing For river training sessions rowers generally train in either Lycra or t-shirts and shorts or leggings or trackies. Tops need to be tight fitting and to have no front pockets (as they catch on the blades). They also need to be the right length, i.e. short, so they don't catch on the runners of the seat when they are rowing.

Food and drink As previously mentioned in the nutrition section, rowers need to bring enough food and drink to ensure that they are able adequately to replenish their nutritional requirements. The amount that they take will depend on the timing of the training and how long the session is. Please refer to the nutrition section (on page 42).

Water bottles Rowers need an endless supply of water bottles – these are often left at the water and not seen again.

Thermos flask A thermos flask is useful for hot drinks (usually to be spilled over clean dry kit in bags rather than consumed).

Sun block, sunglasses and a cap These are for UV protection.

Woolly hat and poggies These are needed for cold weather rowing. It is not possible to row in ordinary gloves.

Waterproofs Rowers should have waterproof leggings or trousers for dry land, and a waterproof top for rowing in if necessary. It is important for rowers to keep dry and warm for as long as possible in cold and wet conditions.

Spare kit Even in good weather conditions the rowers get wet.

Socks Rowers need lots of them. You will end up with odd socks. They get very wet and can be left in kit bags for weeks.

Large towel To dry themselves.

Plastic bag or bin liner For wet or dirty kit before it reaches the washing machine.

Zinc oxide tape and antiseptic cream These are for blisters on hands, knuckle sores and boat bites. You may be asked not to use micropore tape or Elastoplast as these stick to the blades.

Mobile phone – with credit These are usually left turned off or in a remote bag, so contact is impossible when needed.

Rigger jigger Remember to check pockets before kit is washed as these often turn up in the washing machine.

Wellington boots or flip flops Sometimes the rowers will need to walk into the water with their boats. At these times wellies or flip flops are essential.

There are additional items for girls.

Assorted hair ties, head bands, and ribbons To be worn around wrists and hair and then lost or confiscated at school the next day.

Designer t-shirts Girls may ask for these, but get cheapest possible to minimise financial damage.

'Trackies' Keep all outgrown tracksuit bottoms (as they will still fit when worn way below the knickers line as they get older).

Hair brush or comb For back combing pony tail rather than brushing.

Nail file, polish and hand cream There seems to be a vogue for matching nail colour to the racing kit.

Colourful wellies!

Rowers should get into the habit of sorting out their rowing bags both before they go rowing and at the end of sessions. It is surprising how often things are left to fester in the rowing bags after a session, with wet clothes mixed with clean, only to be found seconds before they need to leave for the next session.

A little note about washing kit

Most rowing kit will need to be washed on a cool wash and hand dried, as Lycra will shrink in hot temperatures. This can be an easy and expensive mistake and rather embarrassing to your rower (as it is skin tight already). It is worth telling rowers about this if they are in the habit of doing their own washing or are away on camp and find themselves loading a washing machine for the first time.

What extra kit do the rowers need for events?

Racing kit Coach will tell rowers what specific kit is need for rowing in an event. Normally this will be a team Lycra all in one, racing top and racing leggings. These are usually available from a website and need to be ordered well in advance of the event (as some websites allow you to order on specific dates only). Our experience is that it should be well named and that you should have more than one set, as they may be doing more than one race at an event and if their kit is wet from the first race they will need dry kit for the second. They should look after the rowing kit as it can be very expensive, and it is easy to lose when taken off just before a race.

Safety pins These are also needed to pin the number of the boat onto the clothing on the back of the rower at bow.

Extra clothes These are needed to put on between races, even in summer.

Trainers Rowers should bring these to all events and wear them (on land). They may be asked to bring wellies if it is muddy or to wear when launching the boats.

A little treat In addition to what the rowers need for refuelling, home-made cakes or biscuits are gratefully received by all! It is also a great way of celebrating after what will undoubtedly have been a tough day. If you do not have a keen cook at home, it is not essential for these to be home-made: bought cakes or biscuits that have been taken out of the packet and weathered to look authentically home-made will also do.

Secret diary of a rowing slave

TIME 18.30
DATE Sunday 12 May
SITE Dorney Lake, Berkshire
AIR TEMPERATURE mid teens centigrade
STATUS been here since 8 am so completely knackered
HAIR long since past caring – note to self – remember to book
hairdresser Monday morning
CAFFEINE overdosed and passing urine every 30 minutes

Race begins. Am strategically placed 300m from finish. Calculated this is best spot to watch and give encouragement when crew are starting to tire. Surrounded by other parents. Reassure ourselves that this is right race and that not going to cheer the wrong crew, as at last regatta.

Boats approach. Shouts of encouragement change from scattered slightly self-conscious squawk to a cacophony of screaming banshees. Find myself running along river and zig-zagging to avoid coaches and teenagers on bikes following the race. Lack of fitness starts to tell as guttural screams become whispered whimpers punctuated by breathless gasps for more air. Finishing line approaches. Have completely lost control. Screamed myself hoarse. Race is finished and crew has won. Fake Ray-Bans mist up with tears of joy — what a feeling!

EVENTS

You may have heard about different types of organised rowing events. Your rower could take part in head races, regattas or indoor events. You may also come across bump races and coastal competitions but these are for older rowers.

> **FACT** *The Oxford and Cambridge Boat Race for men started in 1829. The first women's collegiate boat race took place in 1919 between Newnham College, Cambridge, and The London School of Medicine women's crew. The first women's Oxford vs. Cambridge boat race took place in 1927. Henley Royal Regatta started in 1851 and women were first invited to row at this in 1981. In 1988 Henley Women's Regatta was started and is held at Remenham Farm, in Henley. The first men's Head of the River race was in 1926, with the first Women's Head in 1930.* INFORMATION FROM WWW.INSPIREDBYROWING.ORG.UK

What are the main events?

We are listing the main junior national events. However, each club or school will enter smaller regattas or heads, usually in their region. These will vary in size and formality. At the bigger regattas, clubs generally organise marquees and the events will have stalls selling rowing merchandise as well as refreshments. There may be professional photographers with stalls where photographs can be viewed on the day. Head races are usually less formal and parents tend to line up along stretches of the course. Some clubs bring their marquees if there is suitable space on the bank (although these may be to allow the crew to rest or shelter from the weather between divisions rather than for parents).

A SELECTION OF THE MAJOR SCHOOL, CLUB AND GB EVENTS FOR JUNIOR ROWERS

Month	Event	Year group
September		
October	GB rowing trials ergo submissions	Selected J16 up
	The Armada Cup, Switzerland	Selected J15 up
	The Head of the Charles, USA	J15 up
November	GB rowing trials	Selected
December		
January		
February	GB rowing trials	Selected
March	The Scullers Head	Snrs
	Schools' Head of the River	J15 upwards
	The Women's Eights Head of the River	Snrs
	Junior Sculling Head	J14 upwards
	National Junior Indoor Rowing Championships	J11 upwards
April	GB rowing trials	Selected
	Strathclyde Park Regatta	J13 upwards
May	Welsh Open Rowing Championships	J13 upwards
	Munich Junior Regatta	GB
	National Schools Regatta	J14 upwards
	The Gent Regatta, Belgium	J15 upwards
June	Scottish Championships	J13 upwards
	Henley Women's Regatta	Snrs, J16, J15
	GB J16 trials	J16, J15
July	Henley Royal Regatta	U19 upwards
	GB Vs France J16 Match	Selected GB
	National Championships, Nottingham	J14 upwards
	Coupe de la Jeunesse	Selected GB
	Home Countries Regatta	Selected GB
	World Rowing Junior Championships	Selected GB

FACT *The National Schools Regatta started as the Colts and Third Eights Regatta in 1947, with a race between the third eights of Radley, Bedford, Shrewsbury and St Edward's School. In 1964 this event became so large that it was renamed the National Schools Regatta. Girls 4+ were invited to join in 1973 and the girls' events expanded from 1985. It is now the largest domestic rowing event for boys and girls of school age, run over three days with around 3,500 competitors and 50 events.* INFORMATION FROM WWW.NSR.ORG

DETAILS OF THE MAJOR VENUES

Venue	Postcode	Events	Dogs
Cardiff	CF10 5BG	Welsh Open Rowing Championships	yes
Caversham	RG4 SLQ	GB Training Day	no
Dorney Lake	SL4 6QP	The Wallingford Regatta Metropolitan Regatta GB Training Days	yes
Henley	RG9 2LP	Junior Sculling Head Henley Long Distance Sculls Henley Royal Regatta	yes
Remenham Farm, Henley	RG9 3DB	Women's Henley	yes
Nottingham	NG12 2LU	GB Training Days, Camps and Selections * The National Schools Regatta	no no
Strathclyde Park	ML1 3ED	Strathclyde Park Regatta	no
The Tideway London	** **	The Scullers Head The Schools' Head The Women's Head	yes

This event is by invitation only and parents do not attend.

**For London events check the event website for directions and parking.*

Wellies	Paths for bikes	Web address
no	yes	www.walesrowing.com
		www.cardiffcityrc.com
no	coaches only	www.britishrowing.org
no	coaches only	www.dorneylake.com
yes	coaches only	www.henleyrowingclub.org
		www.thescullery.org.uk
		www.hrr.co.uk
yes	coaches only	www.hwr.org.uk
no	coaches only	
no	coaches only	www.nsr.org.uk
no	coaches only	www.scottish-rowing.org.uk
no	yes	www.vrc.org.uk
		www.wsbc.org.uk
		www.wehorr.org

What happens nearer the day?

Coaches will be able to tell you what happens at your club leading up to an event. Essentially, the following will happen:

- rowers will de-rig the boats at the rowing session before an event and the boats will be loaded onto the trailer (unless your club is hosting the event)
- the competitors will know their boats before the event and should have had some training sessions in that specific configuration
- coxes should have checked their equipment and to charge their cox box – they will have been through the course with the coaches and should have a plan of how to navigate the course, which landmarks to watch out for, and should know where the stream changes and best overtaking points are
- coxes will have been asked to download safety and race instructions from the event website and to have made and printed a race plan for the crew
- rowers should also download instructions from the event website and go through their race plan
- as previously mentioned, rowers are encouraged to eat well in the week before an event and possibly to carbohydrate load before big competitions.

We have found the following advice is useful, particularly when your rower is a novice; by the time they reach 18 this should be second nature for all of you:

- make sure the rowers pack their kit bags the day before (this gives them a chance to find that lost top or sock)
- coxes should pack their lifejacket and warm waterproof tops
- making a list beforehand often helps rowers organise themselves on the day – they can start at the time of the race and work backwards (it is surprising how much they need to do in the two hours before racing)

- the most important time for you to know is what time your rower needs to wake up!
- set several alarm clocks in the house to this time
- plan what time your rower needs to have his or her breakfast and when they need to leave the house
- all crew should try to keep up with homework for that weekend (homework books taken to events are often taken for an outing rather than opened)
- make sure your washing machine is free (as it will be overworked and fraught like you after the event)
- consider your diary – events can take all day and are very tiring for everyone involved
- pack you own camera, charge your video and check both have film in them
- charge your phone and load the contact numbers into it in case of emergencies
- make sure you have some small change in your wallet as you may need it for drinks or parking (large notes needed on arrival at some events!)
- de-clutter your car, fill it with petrol and have de-icing spray to hand
- download directions to the event from the event website
- make sure you know what time your rower is competing – it is tragic to travel for two hours and then miss the race by a few minutes
- rowers should try and get enough sleep
- you should try and get enough sleep!

What happens on the day of an event?

Again, we have found the following advice useful:

- you will need to get up early to supervise packed lunches, fill hot flasks, walk the dog, feed the pets … the list is endless

- be prepared to walk on egg shells, as your rower's mood may be affected by nerves
- tell the rest of your family to walk on egg shells, as your own nerves will be shattered!
- in winter months it is likely to be pitch black and cold outside when you wake up, so remember to put on, or bring, your warmest thermal underwear as you will probably feel cold by mid afternoon whatever the weather forecast – multiple layers will keep you warmer and can be more easily removed if the weather warms up later
- your child will need to eat a big breakfast, even if he or she is nervous and doesn't feel like it – porridge or longer lasting cereals, such as weetabix, are good as a minimum
- make sure your rower takes his or her own lunch in their rowing bag as you may not be able to meet up for lunch (and they often prefer to eat with their rowing friends)
- if necessary you will need to drag siblings out of bed and pack them off to see good friends or relatives
- your rower will need to be at the event at least two hours before their race(s). The school or club will probably take a minibus or coach. Rowers often enjoy going to the events in a group, as they can discuss the day, talk to coaches, calm nerves, etc.

What happens when competitors arrive at the event?

The crews need to be at the event at least two hours before they race as they have a number of things to do before they can boat. These include:

- unload the boats from the trailer and rig them – they put them on trestles whilst they do this (this can take about half an hour)
- check the boats for defects (e.g. faulty heel restraints, bow balls, hatch covers)
- sort out the blades and be ready to take them to the water edge before boating

- coxes need to weigh in with the race officials on time (there may be a queue) and have their certificates ready for inspection (they also need to have their life jacket or buoyancy aid)
- rowers need to change into racing kit
- the rower at bow needs to fix the race number to the back of their top and to the bow of the boat
- go to the loo (it sounds obvious but can take longer than expected if the facilities are busy or a long way away)
- have a team talk and go through the race plan, including how to control the boat at start pontoons and stake boats (this often delays the start)
- stretch and warm up (they may go for a run)
- drink
- boat (this can take a while if the trailer is a long way from the boating area and they need to carry the boat through crowds)
- marshal to the start of the race in order (again obvious, but it can take a while to row to the start especially in head races and the boat can be disqualified if it is not there and attached and ready to race on time)
- the coaches need to show their British Rowing race cards to the officials before the start of the race.

How can parents help out at events?

- take competitors to and back from the event
- look after other rowers at an event or to provide hospitality the night before
- sometimes, parents may also be needed to help put up the club's marquee, arrange tables, food and drinks within the tent. The coaches already have their hands full looking after the rowers, the equipment and organising the boats
- offer to be the designated welly catcher!
- afterwards you may well be asked to take the marquee down and pack it away (often harder than putting it up!)

What should parents bring to events?

We have found the following are useful things to bring to events:

Fold-up chairs Typically blue or green and unnamed. Sometimes accidentally upgraded for a newer, smarter or drier model at end of the day.

Rugs or blankets These are useful for the marquee for the rowers to lie on or to keep you warm.

Several layers of clothing and waterproofs In winter, thermal vest and leggings worn under jeans may help prevent hypothermia. Experience has shown that kitten heels or stilettos sink in the mud. Ensure you are carrying as little as possible (designer handbags will not be noticed and may be ruined).

Food It is easy to forget to bring your own food in the rush to get your rower to an event on time. On days like this you can guarantee that the parent next to you is tucking into a feast in very smart Tupperware. Shared food is much more sociable, and for some events (e.g. National Schools) this will be formally organised in advance. A breakfast of bacon, eggs, toast and coffee cooked on a camping stove is a real treat. Extra food for the coaches is very welcome.

Hot drinks (coffee, tea, hot chocolate) These are better at keeping you warm than alcohol and you will be less likely to volunteer for that complicated fundraising event.

Reading or magnifying glasses Even if you do not usually need them. The print in the programme is often so small that you will not be able to read it without them.

Binoculars These ensure that you yell for the correct crew. Discerning parents can spot crews at a distance by their Lycra and the colour of the blades.

Camera or video These are essential kit for fathers. Make sure that batteries are charged the night before. Additionally check you are videoing the correct crew (as they all surprisingly similar and it can be an embarrassing mistake when you play the footage back to your darling or their doting grandparents later on).

Contents of a chemist's shop Include Paracetamol to eliminate your mid-afternoon stress-induced headache and Ibuprofen for your rower's muscle aches and pains. Loo roll is a good idea, as it always seems to run out by mid afternoon.

Directions and race programme The race programme enables you to feel important and to join in with conversations about the event. Experienced parents bring theirs in plastic wallets to ensure protection from the inevitable rain.

How to avoid embarrassing your rower(s) at events

Apart from the obvious (do not go!) we have been advised that blending into the background is essential:

- do not park your sports car on the grass near your school or club's marquee
- never arrive at the event wearing clothing that make you look like an ageing rower – no Lycra, fluorescent rain wear or embarrassing hats/head gear. Large sunglasses will hide bags under the eyes)
- do not stand and chat in the boating area or ignore the calls of 'boat coming through' from crews carrying their boats to and from the water. You may find that you are standing here without realising it. It is tempting to rush down and welcome your rower off the water
- never attempt to hug your child, or show affection in public when they are in their racing gear at events

- do know what position your rower is in the boat (they look surprisingly similar when they are on the water – for girls it helps to know whether their ponytail is blonde or brown)
- if you are bringing your bicycle try not to ride alongside the crews in the manner of a coach as that will be considered very un-cool (and seriously, if you do decide to ride alongside the coaches, make sure that you do not yell your own instructions to the crews – your shouts may disrupt the coaches' genuine instructions)
- do not bring your stop watch
- do not bring a megaphone, however tempting
- do not wander off during an event (for newspaper, coffee or ablutions) without checking the programme first. Races are over in a matter of minutes and it is certain that you will miss your child's only race (which is embarrassing).

Shouting etiquette

It can be tempting to get carried away with yelling encouragement to your rower as they speed past you. After all, you have all had a very long build up to the event and it is usually over in a matter of minutes. This might seem to be a natural way to show support and interest.

However, shouting encouragement such as 'you're winning' whilst they are rowing to the start of the race is embarrassing to your offspring and even more so if it is mistakenly aimed at the wrong crew.

Similarly, during the race, shouting encouragement like 'crack on' or 'you're nearly there' is likely to be met with distain. It is better to shout for your rower's boat club rather than to call your child's name and to support all rowers from your club.

Generally, you will find that groups of parents from one club will sit or stand together along the bank. Groups of parents yelling together can make quite an effective din. Often, this will lead to friendly rivalry on the banks between different clubs, which can help to pass the time!

How can you tell if the race is going well?

The following can be a helpful quick guide to know how your rower's boat is fairing during the race.

- do they look any good? Does the stroke cycle look smooth and seamless? Good technique is more important than a high stroke rate
- are all the rowers in time with each other? They should all be following the rate set by the stroke
- is there alot of splashing? If the blades are entering the water correctly then the catches should be clean with minimal splashing
- is the boat going at a constant speed? It should not jerk, which might indicate that the rowers are out of time with each other
- have they been overtaken? Crews can start out of order at Head Races or Processionals and sometimes the names of crews are muddled up.

Swans, ducks and geese

Very occasionally a crew will find that they are rowing into a flock of birds on the course. You might expect that the birds would move with the commotion of the oncoming boats, but if they are tame they might not. Swans are protected birds and are unlikely to be moved off the course by race officials during a race. So warn your young rowers!

FACT *Swans are protected under a 1592 act, introduced by Henry VIII which makes it illegal to injure or kill any swan. In 1992 a man was jailed for three months under this act!*

What happens after the racing has finished?

Parents and rowers should remember to be gracious in defeat and humble in victory. You should thank the coaches for their hard work, whatever the results!

As a parent it is tempting to go home as soon as your rower has raced. However, it is important to support all the rowers from your club. Coaches often welcome help from parents with taking down the marquee.

For the rowers the event ends when the boat trailer is loaded. The boats need to be de-rigged and loaded onto the boat trailer. The rowers should do this. Expect this to take at least an extra 30 minutes (longer when they stand around and chat and the parents do the same). Watching the trailer being loaded is quite a spectacle, as it requires precision and skill. No rower should leave until this is complete.

Remember that your child will be exhausted after an event and the journey home may be quiet. They may have been building up to the event for weeks beforehand, and will have rowed at least double the length on the programme (as they have rowed to the start). It is a very long day.

Photography and videos

Your club may have its own policy on photography, so it is best to ask your coach. Many schools and clubs encourage parents to take photographs, as these can be shared or put on the club's website. Videos of the crews taken by parents are invaluable to the coaches, as they can use them as teaching aids later on. Occasionally, clips of the bigger events are posted on the internet, and are fun to watch.

Many events have event photographers who will take photos of all crews and these can be viewed and ordered online. You will need to know the race number and the class of boat.

How do you find out the results?

For head races, rowers will not know how they have done until all the boats in their race have completed the course. Sometimes rowers in the same race will be placed in a different division, so it may appear that your son or daughter has won by the results posted before lunch, only to find that someone is faster in the afternoon division (don't start celebrating too early).

The times and therefore the results for each race are available on the event website, usually that evening or the following day. You will need to know the race name and number in order to find your rower's times. The results are listed in full (i.e. sequentially regardless of class) as well as in divisions (a glass of wine in the comfort of your own home helps).

Regatta results are usually announced as the competition unfolds. The results of heats are posted on boards, either in alphabetical order if it is a processional or by time order. The final results are announced at the end of the race – as a spectator on the water's edge it can difficult to see who has won at the end of a close race. The full results are listed similarly to the table below and are usually available online the next day. At larger events, the results can be accessed as they happen using the internet (see www.mikrotime.com). Weather conditions can affect the boat times on a given course. Tail winds make times faster and head winds or cross winds will slow boats down. This can be difficult if conditions change rapidly during an event.

A RESULTS TABLE

DIVISION1. Race 4 WJ14 8+

Position	No	Crew	A/B	Time	Margin *	m/s
1	104	XXXX	A	12.20	0	4.1
2	97	XXXX	A	12.52.9	32.9	3.9
3	99	XXXX	A	13.08	48.4	3.8

* This is the winning margin in seconds

Prizes

Prizes may be awarded to the winners alone, or they may be for the first three placed boats. Some races have a cup in addition to individual medals. The winning crew can take these back to their clubs for the year. All this will be clear in the events programme, which will also detail the history behind the prizes. These accounts are well worth reading.

At head events, the award ceremony is usually at the end of the day when racing has finished. During regattas, the prizes may be given out at the end of the final race for each event. This is usually from a pontoon and the crew line up alongside and receive their prizes whilst still seated in the boats. Find out where this is if there is a possibility that your child will receive a prize. These ceremonies happen very promptly after the finish of the race and you could find yourself miles away. Otherwise, there may be an award ceremony at the end, on land, when racing has finished.

FACT *The first competitive boat race took place in Venice in 1315. Most early boat races were as a result of wagers between competitors. The first professional sculling championships were in London in 1831. Nowadays, prizes are no longer wagers, but take the form of medals, cups, shields, tankards and sometimes sculls!* INFORMTION FROM: WWW.INSPIREDBYROWING.ORG.UK

British Rowing race cards (previously know as ARA cards)

Your child might mention that he or she has a British Rowing race card. These look like driving licences and contain the following details: the rower's name, date of birth, their photograph, their British Rowing membership number, their club, the date of issue and expiry and their sculling and rowing points (each card has JA, JB, JM and then 1–12 sculling and 1–12 rowing printed around the edge of the card. Cards are punched over these marks when the rowers win races).

Race cards are usually kept by the coaches who bring them to events, so parents may never see one (you may have noticed your head coach clutching on to what usually looks like a very battered photograph album. It is very important that they do not lose this as rowers may not race without their cards).

EVENTS

Rowers need to show their race cards to the officials at the start of the race and at the end if they win. The cards ensure that the same person on the entry form is rowing in an event and act as a record of that rower's achievements.

British Rowing has changed the points system as from April 1 2009. The points system is there to make races fairer, each category of race will have entry criteria, and if a rower has too many points they cannot enter that race (this mainly applies to senior events).

Junior rowers start with 0 points and for wins at qualifying competitions from the J16 level upwards they will earn 1 rowing (sweeping) or sculling point per win. There is a new J17 category of race. If your rower is competing at the World Rowing Junior Championships they will automatically earn 6 points. The maximum points that can be earned are 12. Promising junior rowers may expect to have one or two points from the age of 16, depending on their successes.

Rowing or sculling points for individual rowers in a crew are added together to make up the points for that crew (depending on whether it is a sweeping or sculling event). This will dictate which category of event they can enter in senior competitions such as Henley or the Head of the River races.

Points are added at the end of an event, so if your rower is in two races ('doubling') and gains points in the first one, his or her rating will not change until after the second race.

It is the responsibility of the rower or coach to update the points on the British Rowing register and on the rower's card.

Last-minute changes to crews

British Rowing has strict rules about changes to crews before and during events. Before an event, up to half the crew and the cox may switch as long as it is before the first race and the new rowers are from the same club and all have licences to row. The swapped-in cox may come from a different club. Once racing has started, a crew may not switch rower or cox without the authority of the event organisers. This might be due to injury or illness, in which case the rower or cox who is unfit or ill will be seen by an official before they can stand down. If a boat wins an event with unofficial crew they may be disqualified.

Why bother?

Nothing can prepare you for the exhilaration you will feel at seeing your son or daughter rowing past. This is as true for the first outing when your child is a novice to when they are in the first eight. What your school or boat club achieves during this journey is extraordinary. There is often a great social life for parents and rowers alike. Fathers and mothers can become equally involved from the banks of a river or a reservoir. You meet new friends, share experiences and have great fun. Life-long friendships are forged amongst the rowers and parents.

Rowers have to be mentally focused to be able to row. They generally become very organised with their studies in order to fit in the long hours of training. It is no surprise, therefore, that many rowers achieve stunning exam results. They become fantastically fit and many of them will excel at other sports because of this supreme fitness.

The athletes learn a great deal about themselves through rowing. They learn to become team players and to put personal ambition aside when racing in a crew.

'… Reflect on your experiences and accomplishments. Remember the dedication, the pain, the jubilation, the camaraderie, your family. Remember the feel of the oar in your hand, the swing, the perfect catch, the pull, the drive and the run of the boat beneath you. But most importantly, never forget the glory is not in you or any individual. Instead, remember that the glory is always in the team.'

JOE BLASKO, NOVICE COACH, ST IGNATIUS HIGH SCHOOL, CLEVELAND 1996–97.

However:

- forget lie-ins
- forget family weekends away (you/your son or daughter will either be at an event or training for one)
- weekends take on a new structure for the whole family, and it can be difficult to manage the rowing drop off and pick ups, particularly if you have other busy children

- there is a lot of hanging around for parents whether it is after training sessions or at an event (at the events do not expect to see or have a lot of contact with your rower – they become very focused and often prefer the company of their fellow competitors)
- do not expect feedback from your son or daughter after sessions, or events – if lucky, you may get a grunt (they are extremely tired)
- your rower's mood at weekend lunch will depend on the how the training session goes (be careful when accepting invitations out to lunch!)
- after a good session or event they may be elated, and talk too fast in rowing language that you don't understand; after a session that goes less well, expect tears (and a blow-by-blow account of what went wrong and why it wasn't fair)
- your washing machine will be on most of the time

Despite all the above, rowing becomes totally addictive. What these rowers achieve is awesome.

'For the rest of your life you will always be able to say I was a member of a very special team whose whole was greater than the sum of its parts and it was one of the greatest experiences of my life.' ANON.

ROWING ESSENTIAL FACTS

The following are the essentials to know in order to be able to conduct a conversation about rowing without making a complete fool of yourself.

Sweeping and sculling

It is very easy to be confused by these terms. In a rowing boat they have one blade and in a sculling boat they have two.

When the novices start 'rowing' they are actually 'sculling' as they have two blades. Sculling puts equal pressure on the back on both sides, and so the athletes learn sculling until they have finished growing (this is generally the J15 level). Older rowers will then be taught how to row using a single blade, which is called 'sweeping' or 'sweep oaring'. If the blade is held to the left side of the body, this is bow side, and if it is to the right it is stroke side. The crew will usually have their blades on alternate sides in sweeping boats. However, the pattern can be different if rowers at certain positions in the boats are stronger on one side (for example, you could have a stroke, bow, stroke, bow, bow, stroke, bow, stroke configuration).

When you are standing on the bank watching your child rowing, as they approach you and have their back to you, if they are in bow position the blade will be on their left. As the boat passes you, they are facing you; the same blade will now be on your right (and vice versa). It can be very confusing!

Blades

Your club's blades (oars) will have their own design on the paddle. This makes it easier to recognise the boat from a distance. Each blade has a red or green stripe on it near the handle, so that the rowers know which blade to use in each hand. The bow blades are green and the stroke blades are red.

Rowing blades are larger and heavier than sculling blades and have bigger spoons. Boys' blades are longer than girls' blades and are therefore heavier. The blades are categorised by letters, for example A, B, C, D, E, F, etc., according to their age. There is little logic to how they are named and even the coaches can get confused. Rowers will use different blades depending on which boat they are in. Each member of the crew needs to use the same lettered blade.

The different positions in the boat

The rower at the front of the boat (as it moves) is called the bow. Whilst racing, the bow will normally wear the number of the boat on his or her back. Depending on the type of boat, the rowers in the middle of the boat are sometimes described as the 'powerhouses' and tend to have the strongest pull in the water. The rower sitting nearest to the back of the boat is called the stroke. He or she will set the rhythm for the crew.

Scull ranking, seat races, doubles matrix and pairs matrix

As we have mentioned before, finding the best crew is not as easy as it may seem to a non-rower. If you take eight rowers and put them together in a boat, the boat may be faster than you would expect from their individual times, on the other hand it may be slower.

There are several reasons for this. Some rowers suit certain types of boat, some are better technically, others are physically stronger, some are better team players and others do well because they are so determined. Each of these factors plays a part in how well a particular formation will work and how fast the boat will be on the water.

> 'Rowing is an endurance test that finishes at a speed of up to 10 meters per second. Crews cover the middle 1000 meters at about 40 strokes per minute, but, over the first and last 500 meters, shift up a gear to as many as 47.'

INFORMATION FROM: WWW.OLYMPICS.ORG.UK

There are four types of races that most clubs use in order to help tease out the best combinations. These are sculling ranking, seat races, pairs matrix and doubles matrix. The following are explanations of what these are, but it is then the coach's decision as to how the results are used.

Sculling ranking is when the rowers are put into singles and raced over a set distance. They are ranked on their times.

Seat races are used to assess places in fours or eights. The coaches arrange timed races where two coxed fours row against each other over a set distance. They are coxed so that the steering of one rower does not affect the times of the rest of that crew. The coaches will then swap two of the crew from one boat to the other and note the effect over the same distance.

Pairs matrix races are used to assess places in eights, fours and pairs. Rowers might race in fours as well as pairs and the times of different combinations are recorded. They may also be rotated so that the bow and stroke swap sides, to see the effect of this (some rowers are better on one side). The times of the different combinations are recorded. It does not always follow that the two fastest pairs will make the fastest four, etc.

Doubles matrix races are used to assess places in quads and doubles. They are similar to the pairs races, except they are sculling and so there is no need to swap bow and stroke sides.

Somehow at the end of all this, the coaches are able to work out the best combinations for the boats. Some rowers are better at singles, some work better in a crew, and some are better at sweeping than sculling. Leaving someone out of a crew must be one of the most difficult parts of coaching. Fortunately, many events have lots of different categories enabling each rower to find their niche.

At both regattas and head races, the coaches may be restricted by their choice of crews depending on the timetabling of different categories. It may be that there is not enough time for your rower to get from the finish of one race to the start of another in a regatta. In a head race, all boats in one division need to be lined up at the start before the race begins so they cannot row in two boats in the same division. Additionally, they may be restricted by the total number of British Rowing points that the crew has, which means they cannot enter a particular race.

Head races

These run from October until March or April. Head races are time trials run over distances between 3000m to 7500m. They are longer courses than at regattas, and only a single race. They test endurance (the hours spent rowing up and down on the water and the hours spent on the ergos come in to play here).

The crews row down to the start and are then lined up by race officials called marshals. All crews in that division have to reach the start before any boats can start to race. The slower boats are usually sent to the start first, but the faster boats will usually race first (so singles will race after doubles or quads). Before the race starts, each crew will have rowed down all or most of the course (this is very exciting and nerve racking to watch if your son or daughter is a novice or in a single for the first time, as you may wonder whether he or she can make it to the start).

The boats sometimes have to wait at the start for a considerable length of time before they are called to race. This is particularly true for novice crews as they are sent to the start first but may race at the end of that division. Thus it is important that they have enough clothing with them, which can be removed quickly and stored in the boat (without capsizing!). They may also need a small drink and a last-minute snack with them.

Each boat gets underway when their number is called and they row across the start line. The timing of the race starts when they cross the time line, which they should do at full speed. This is called a rolling start. The next crew is then prepared and sent down between 5–20 seconds later. There is usually a slight gap between divisions and also for lunch.

As there is only a small time gap between boats at the start of the race, it is usual for boats to overtake each other on the course. The slower boat must get out of the way of the overtaking boat (you can get an idea of how well your crew is doing by looking at the numbers of the boats around them). Because of the difference in speed between coxed and coxless boats, and sculling or sweeping boats, you cannot compare the times of boats of different types.

The crews row the course according to their race plan. They might for example take ten fast strokes at the beginning, then settle to a consistent race pace and then take the rate up at the end. The coaches are able to judge how fast the crews are going by using a stopwatch to calculate their stroke rate.

On some stretches of some rivers the current is strong, so the precise line taken by the boat can make a big difference to the overall time. Good coxing can make a huge difference.

The races have race marshals in rescue boats monitoring the course. This is important as the courses are long and you may not be able to see down the whole length of the course from the bank. If a crew capsizes they will be picked up and taken to the finish in a speedboat to prevent hypothermia. Crews will have been taught how to capsize safely, and should all have a spare set of clothing and a towel with them in their bags (see section on capsizing on page 56).

Regattas

The regatta seasons starts in April. Regattas are side-by-side races, with the boats racing in lanes, with up to eight boats racing alongside each other. The boats start at the same time (as in the Olympics).

The races are divided into heats, and the heats lead up to a final. If there are lots of boats entered in the race, there may be a processional race before the side-by-side heats (this is like a head race and starts with a rolling start; here the rowers row up to a time line and aim for full speed at the start line). At these a certain number of boats will go through to the next round. For example, in a race with 24 crews, the first 18 may go through to the heats.

Depending on the number of heats, there may be a repechage. This means that the runners up from the heats race together and then the winner of this heat gains a place in the final. The crew that wins the repechage will have raced one more heat than the other boats. It is possible that your rower's boat will beat a boat in a heat and then find that they have to race them again in the final.

The lanes in the centre are usually for the fastest boats in the heats so that at the finish there is likely to be an inverted V shape. (If the course is very windy or there is a strong current this may not happen, in which case the fastest boats are given the lane with the best advantage.)

'When I was with Steve, we reckoned we could get up to top speed in about a month.' QUOTATION FROM: *A LIFETIME IN A RACE* MATTHEW PINSENT
© EBURY PRESS

At regattas where there are fewer entries in an event than there are lanes e.g. four boats entered into an event with five lanes, there will be a heat for lanes before the final, and the fastest boat is given the best lane. This is instead of a straight final where the luck of the draw dictates which crew has the lane advantage. This is one reason why crews that have a clear lead in a heat will still row to the end in good time, in order to secure a good lane in the next round (it is tempting to shout 'slow down!' so they save their energy for later).

Regatta races are shorter than head races: the standard length is 2000m but they can be 500m. So the start is important. The crews row down to the start of the race, and then manoeuvre into their starting positions. This takes practice and can be difficult for novice rowers. The boats line up at the starting pontoons with the bow facing down the course. The coxes have to keep the boats straight and there is usually a race assistant who holds the boat at the stake boat. Coxless crews obviously do this themselves, with the bow rower steering. If it is windy it can be difficult to line the boats up to the stake boats, particularly if the crews are inexperienced or the boats are eights or octs. In this situation, there will be a 'free start'. Here, the boats line up at the start as straight as possible but are not held to the stake boat.

The starter calls the names of each crew, and when all boats are ready the starter raises the red flag, calls 'Attention' and then, if all the boats remain aligned, drops the red flag shouting 'Go'.

The first stroke is very important. The crews will row according to their race plan, going off fast, settling into a cruising speed or stride and then winding it up to the finish. Coxless crews should remember to focus on their own race and not look at their rival crews otherwise they may steer off course at this stage.

The umpire follows the crews down the course in a launch. The umpire can stop a race by raising a red flag. If a crew is veering out of their lane, or heading for an obstacle, such as a bank or tree, the umpire will use a white flag. The umpire will call to the boat whilst pointing the white flag in the direction in which they should move.

Generally the crews will be rowing at a faster rate than in head races as the distance is shorter. These races will be over more quickly than head races and may only take a few minutes. They are therefore easier to miss.

If your rower's crew is knocked out, then the whole event is over very quickly. However, try to stay until all the crews in your boat club have finished so that you can cheer them on.

Indoor rowing competitions

There are a growing number of indoor rowing competitions and indoor rowing is becoming a separate sport with regional competitions leading to national events.

Rowers will do either a set time on an ergo machine or a set distance – for example, 2 minutes for J12, 3 minutes for J13, 4 minutes for J14 and 5 minutes for J15 – and their distances are recorded. J16 or seniors might do a set distance (2km) the first to that distance wins. They are usually held in a gym or hall, and a large number of ergo machines are linked to central screens. The competitors start as if in a race and the central screen shows tiny boats in different lanes, so all can see how they are faring. These competitions are intense and noisy and surprisingly tiring for spectators!

Negotiating the event programme

There is an art to understanding a rowing event's programme as there is all sorts of information hidden on the page. You might find it difficult to identify which race your son or daughter is in. This is because the events are listed in shorthand and there are numerous possibilities.

Broadly speaking there are four things that influence the event categories:

- age
- type of boat
- whether the boat is coxed
- whether it is an open event (i.e. allows both sexes), a women or men only event or a mixed event.

There are three age differentials:

- junior (under 18 on 1 September of that year)
- senior (including novice, lightweights and U23)
- veteran (over 31 in the year of event).

Juniors

It is likely that your rower will be entered into junior events. British Rowing defines a junior by their age on 1 September of that year. So J13, 14, 15, 16 and 18 must not be 13, 14, 15, 16 or 18 by the 1 September in the year preceding the event. Upper sixth formers can row in junior events until the day before their 19th birthday, so long as they are still at school. Juniors in the WJ14 or J14 age group are not allowed to race in sweeping events.

At junior level, the events may be divided into A or B classes – where crews that have won a certain amount of events that year are not allowed to enter B races.

Coxes of junior crews must be under 18, but can be older than the boat class. They have a minimum weight restriction of 50kg for J18 and J16 events and 45kg for J15 or under. They need to use weights to increase their weight to these figures if necessary. This is called 'dead weight'. They must wear a buoyancy aid in the boat.

Junior maiden events are for juniors in the J15 and above age groups who have not yet won any qualifying junior or senior events.

At Great Britain U18 selection level, the age is taken from the rower's age on the 31 December rather than 1 September. For the U16 GB France event, rowers must be over 14 years of age and under 16 on 1 September of the preceding year. All selected rowers have to show their passports.

Seniors

The next age group is U23, where the oarsmen and coxes must be under 23 on 31 December. At senior level, senior A is open to all competitors. Senior B is for those under 23 before 1 January.

Lightweight events are held where men must not exceed 72.5kg and women 59kg. The average weight of the lightweight crew (excluding the cox) must not exceed 70kg for men and 57kg for women. There is a lightweight Oxford and Cambridge Women's Boat Race.

Veterans

In the UK, British Rowing define a veteran as a rower who has reached 31 at the end of the calendar year. This age varies between countries. A crew for a veteran race must all be veterans, except the cox. The average age of the crew is important and determines which class the boat is in. Veteran races are divided into classes ABCDEFGHI with different lower average age limits. For example, Class A has an average age restriction of 31 whereas class I has an average age restriction of 75. A boat may have three 31year olds in it and only one rower who is 56, so that the presence of the older rower will alter the boat class for that crew, changing it from an A class to a C class. In this way, older rowers become valued members of the team.

'Today, I broke my world record by three seconds. What I was trying to do was to break 8.00 but I didn't quite manage it, but that leaves something to look forward to. Although I don't know, at 81 years old I think that you're supposed to be going downhill instead of uphill ...'

JOE CLINARD, 2000 CRASH – B COMPETITOR (STILL SETTING RECORDS AGED 90)

AGE CATEGORIES

Boat class	Abbreviation
J12–J18	Junior boys, under 12–18
WJ12–WJ18	Junior girls, under 12–18
WS1–S4	Women's senior classes 1–4
S1–S4	Men's senior classes 1–4
WSE	Women's single elite
SE	Men's single elite
VA–VI	Veterans' classes A to I
N	Novice men
WN	Novice women
WLE	Women's lightweight elite
LE	Men's lightweight elite

Type of boat

Here too there are many sub-categories depending on the number of rowers in the boat – i.e. one, two, four or eight – and whether the boats are sculling or sweeping. You will need to know which type of boat your rower is in to find out their race.

In sculling boats the rowers use two blades and in sweeping boats one blade. On the programme 'x' denotes a sculling boat.

Sweeping boats have different names from sculling boats. – for example, an eight not an oct or octuple and a four not a quad, and a pair rather than a double. Yet another thing to remember!

Whether there is a cox is denoted by '**+**' or '**–**'. Some boats always have a cox – for example, an octuple and so the + sign may be omitted.

An example of a boys' programme is shown on the next page. In girls' events a '**W**' is added to the event class to denote a female crew e.g. WJ18.

AN EXAMPLE OF A BOYS' EVENT PROGRAMME

Boat type	Code	Event class	Boat	How it will appear in the programme
Rowing	8+	J18	An eight, coxed	J18 8+
	4+	J18	Coxed four	J18 4+
	4-	J16	Coxless four	J16 4-
	2-	J18	Coxless pair	J18 2-
Sculling	8x	J14	Octuple scull, coxed	J14 8x
	4x+	J13	Coxed quadruple scull	J13 4x
	4x	J16	Coxless quad	J16 4x
	2x	J15	Double scull	J15 2x
	1x	J15	Single scull	J15 1x

Divisions

On the programme, the divisions denote the section of the event. Each division will have an approximate start time. There is usually a break between divisions.

Naming of crews

Boats may be named A, B, C depending on the number of boats in each event from your school or club. Only the name of the rower at bow is printed in the programme and each boat is assigned a number, which the rower at bow wears on his or her back. This makes it easier for their times to be recorded. The boats also have the number on their bow, so that it makes it easier to recognise them as they fly by.

Lanes

At regattas the boats race side–by–side in lanes and the programme should show which bank the lanes are numbered from.

The programme at head races

EXAMPLE PROGRAMME FOR A HEAD RACE

All crews please marshal on the BERKSHIRE* side of the river

Boat No	Division	Club	Event	Name
1	1	xxxx	WJ14 8X	xxxx
2	1	xxxx	WJ14 8X	xxxx

*The crews row down to the start on this side of the river and race down to finish on the opposite side

BOATING TIMES: DIVISION 1

Boat number	Time**
1-20	8.30am to 9.00am
21-40	10.00am to 10.15am
41-60	9.15am to 9.30am

**Note that the boat times may not be in the expected order

The programme at regattas

The style of the racing at regattas will depend on the width of the water stretch. In narrower waters, the races may be side-by-side, and in larger events there may be several lanes.

EXAMPLE PROGRAMME FOR A REGATTA WITH TWO LANES

Race No	Time	Event	Crew Bucks*	Crew Berks*	Winner to race	Loser to race
1	08.15	J18 4-	41	42	35	50
2	08.20	J18 4-	43	44	51	35
3	08.25	J18 4-	45	46	35	52

*Only two lanes for racing so event takes longer

EXAMPLE PROGRAMME FOR A REGATTA WITH FIVE LANES

WJ18 4-
Race number 1

Lane1) xxxx
Lane2) xxxx
Lane3) xxxx   First 3 to semi final race 10
Lane4) xxxx
Lane5) xxxx

EXAMPLE PROGRAMME FOR A REGATTA WITH FIVE LANES

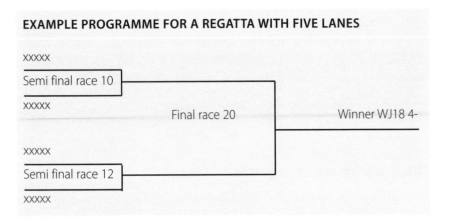

A PARENT'S GUIDE TO ROWING

Composite Crews

These are crews made up of rowers from different clubs These will be written with the names of the clubs divided by a comma e.g. X, Y, Z. At J16 level and above, these may consist of GB rowing crews who are practising for an international event. At younger ages these may be made up of clubs combining rowers to make up a boat.

APPENDIX

Boat structure

1 Stern
2 Bow and Bow ball

3 Sling
4 Trestle

1 Handle
2 Collar

3 Spoon

1 Rigger	5 Steering wire
2 Swivel	6 Runner
3 Pin	7 Gunwales or saxboard
4 Gate	

1 Runner	3 Position of seat at frontstops
2 Seat	4 Position of seat at backstops

A rower's meal guide

Breakfast

- Cereal with semi-skimmed milk or porridge with a small amount of brown sugar or jam (an average bowl is approximately 60g made with 200ml semi-skimmed milk)
- 2 slices wholemeal toast or 3 crumpets with honey or jam
- Fruit juice to drink

Lunch suggestions

One of the following:

- 1 wholemeal roll or 4 slices of bread with chicken/tuna/hummus/egg and salad
- Lentil soup with wholemeal roll
- 2 pieces of toast or a baked potato (approximately 175g potato gives 50g carbohydrates) and baked beans
- Pasta with tomato sauce and vegetables (225g of cooked pasta gives 50g of carbohydrate and the source will provide additional carbohydrate and protein)

Followed by:

- Fruit
- Low fat yoghurt

Supper suggestions

One of the following:

- Lasagne (made with mince with less than 5% fat)
- Stir-fried chicken with noodles and vegetable
- Baked potato with baked beans (approximately 175g potato gives 50g carbohydrates)
- Salmon with boiled potatoes and vegetable
- Pasta with ratatouille (225g of cooked pasta gives 50g of carbohydrate and the source will provide additional carbohydrate and protein)
- Bean chilli with rice
- Macaroni cheese

With one of more of the following vegetables:

- 15g of carrots (gives approximately 3g of carbohydrates and 0.5g of protein)
- 85g of peas (gives approximately 16g of carbohydrates and 0g protein)
- 85g of courgettes (gives 2g of carbohydrates and 2g of protein)

Then a pudding such as:

- Rice pudding and jam
- Jelly and custard
- Fruit crumble and custard

50g carbohydrate snack ideas

Bread
- 2–3 slices malt loaf
- 2 slices of wholemeal bread
- 1 bagel
- 3 crumpets
- 1–2 currant buns

Cakes and biscuits and sweets
- 2 fruit scones
- 3 jam tarts
- 5 plain digestives
- 4–5 fig rolls
- 10 rice cakes
- 8 fingers Kit Kat
- 1 Mars bar
- 2 cereal bars (check on the labels)
- 2 tubes fruit pastilles

Fruit:
- 4 apples
- 4 oranges
- 2 large bananas
- 75g raisins

Each of the above provides 50g of carbohydrate. It is best to eat a mixture of these. It is interesting to see how much of some of these your rower needs to eat in order to refuel.

INFORMATION FROM: JULIET WILSON MSc NUTRITIONAL MEDICINE, SENR

Core stability exercises

Do each exercise for 50 seconds then allow 10 seconds to change to next exercise. Remember to breathe! There are three levels starting with level one in the left hand column and progressing to level three on the right.

Front plank
Min of 90 sec
Good = 3 min

Front plank
Lift one leg. Hold 2 sec.
Change

Front plank
Lift one leg and extend alt arm. Hold 2 sec change.

Side plank
Elbow down.
Maintain pelvis stability

Side plank
Arm straight.
Maintain pelvis stability

Side plank
Arm straight. One leg and one arm raised.
Maintain pelvis stability

4 point kneel
Raise arm. Change.
Maintain pelvis stabilty

4 point kneel/Superman
Raise arm and extend alt leg.
Maintain pelvis stabilty

4 point kneel on foam roll
Raise arm and extend alt leg.
Maintain pelvis stabilty

Single leg raises
Maintain pelvis stabilty
Slow and controlled. Touch hand to knee for variation

Reverse crunch
Feet touch floor then lift to 90 degree/parallel to floor

Raise body and knees
Not a curl. Slow and controlled. NB: Breath, long and deep

Single leg raises
Raise one straight leg
5 inches. Change

Single leg raises
Raise both legs (straight).
Hold and then touch floor

Lift pelvis
Raise legs straight. Lift pelvis
towards ceiling

Legs raised body lift
Raise both legs, straight.
Lift body

Bent knee wipers
Raise both knees bent at 90
degrees. Rotate left and right

Windscreen wipers
Raise legs to 90 degrees.
Move legs from side to side

V-sit and hold
Sit and hold posture

V-sit and twist
Rotate but maintain posture
and stability

V-sit and twist with ball
Rotate but maintain posture
and stability

Bridging
Lift pelvis so that knees,
pelvis and shoulders are in a
straight line

Bridging and hold
Lift pelvis so that knees,
pelvis and shoulders are in a
straight line. Hold

**Bridging and single leg
marching**
Lift pelvis so that knees,
pelvis and shoulders are in a
straight line. Lift one foot
5cm then change

**Bridging and single leg
extended**
Lift pelvis so that knees,
pelvis and shoulders are in a
straight line. Keep single leg
extended

**Bridging and single leg
extended. Hold**
Lift pelvis so that knees,
pelvis and shoulders are in a
straight line. Keep single leg
extended

Sit-ups
With one leg straight and
other bent, lift shoulders off
ground (keep head in
alignment). Hold for 5 deep
breaths

Rower's language

A

above heads an instruction given to the crew to lift the boat from the shoulders to above the head, holding the boat by one hand on each sax board

awesome your son or daughter's new favourite word (after 'like') – generally means brilliant, great, wonderful, etc.

B

back it down an instruction given by a cox to the crew to push the blade through the water towards the stern (used to turn boat around)

backsplash the water that splashes behind the rower (it is what can make the rower behind very wet)

backstops the finish of a stroke, with legs straight and oar handle against the body

blade what non-rowers would call an oar

boat bite cuts to the calf caused by the seat metal

boat seat a rubber cushioned seat to put onto the fitted boat seat to aid comfort, to improve technique or to convert a boy's seat to a girl's seat in a composite crew

bow the front of the boat, i.e. the end that is coming first in the race; also refers to the person sitting at the front of the boat when it is moving (rather than calling them number one)

bow ball rubber ball on the tip of the bow to minimize injury in the event of a collision; it is also used to work out who crosses the line first in closely fought races

bow blade the blade held on the left of the body; it has a green stripe on it near the handle

bow number the number that the bow wears to identify the boat in a race

breakfast the most important meal of the day and still on the table when you get back from an event

British Rowing formally known as the ARA (Amateur Rowing Association)

C

calls the instructions to the crew made during a piece or race

canvas covering enclosing the bow and stern sections of the boat; the term used to describe a leading margin of the crew: 'the length of a canvas', i.e. 2–3m

capsize test test to show that novice rowers can capsize safely and can demonstrate that they can do this according to British Rowing guidelines before they are allowed to row

carb loading an increase in carbohydrate content of a rower's diet the week before a major event

catch the moment a blade enters the water at the beginning of a stroke

catching a crab when the blades catch in the water with the result that it is difficult to catch up with other crew members before the next stroke, and the blades clash

circuits tortuous gym exercises to improve fitness

circulation plan shows the route that boats should take at events when entering the water, rowing up to the start, racing and leaving the water – there is usually a practice circulation pattern and a racing one

cleaver the most common type of blade (oar) – they are usually fibreglass and hollow, so are very light

coach the person in charge of your son or daughter whilst rowing and the person who will teach your rower all aspects of rowing (to be respected)

composite crew a crew put together from different clubs – can be both male and female (your rower may find that they are racing against a composite crew that together make up the GB team. They can be hard to beat!)

core stability exercises that build up the core muscles of your abdomen, which help to protect your lower back and improve your balance

cox/coxswain the most important member of the crew

cox box the gadget used to show the cox the stroke rate – it also connects the microphone to the boat's speaker system

D

dead heat at a regatta when two or more crew cross the finish line simultaneously (the Chief Judge may declare an immediate re-row between these crews or if the timetable allows, they will all go through to the next round; at a head race, identical times will be acknowledged in the place order)

dead weight the extra weight carried by the cox in order bring them to the required target weight for that event

de-rig to remove the riggers and the seat(s) from the shell of the boat – done before boats are loaded onto a trailer

divisions the equivalent to a league in a different sport

double a sculling boat with two rowers using two blades each

doubling is when a rower is entered into 2 events in a competition

drag the resistance on an ergo machine (also the term used to describe getting up before 7am at the weekend)

drop a cox's instruction to the crew to drop their blades into the water

drugs testing there to ensure fairness in sport. For more information look at www.britishrowing.org/antidoping

E

easy there a cox's instruction to the crew, meaning stop rowing whilst the boat glides to a halt, with feathered blades above the water in away position

eight a sweeping boat with eight rowers with one blade each

ergometer (ergo) machine of great torture, used to build up strength and technique. Novice rowers also use them to learn how to row

F

faffing ineffectual bustling – parents and rowers alike do a lot of this!

fall in/out no, not what you think, but either 'start' or 'stop' rowing as a group – if the cox indicates a specific rower, that rower either starts or stops rowing or comes into rhythm with the rest of the crew

false start called by the judge, the race umpire or the starter when a crew or crews start cross the line or start before the official signal of 'Go' (the crew or crews receive an official warning)

feathered blades position of blades when parallel to the water between strokes

final the last decisive race in a category. Regattas have these, head races do not.

finish the end of the stroke cycle – same as backstops and a blessed relief

firm up an instruction to rowers from the cox to apply more pressure.

FISA the body governing world rowing. It is worth visiting their website to read about their excellent core values. www.worldrowing.com

four a sweeping boat with four rowers each with one blade – the boat may be coxed or coxless

free start used in windy conditions when it is not possible to line up boats against the stake boats – boats line up as best they can and then they start

front stops the moment a blade enters the water at the beginning of a stroke (the same as the catch)

full pressure an instruction given by the cox to the crew to give 100% power

G

gate/swivel the swivelling support for the blade, fixed to the rigger – needs to be firmly secured before rowing otherwise the blade can fall out

grunt most usual answer to the question 'Did you have a good session?'

gunwale (pronounced 'gunnel') upper edge of the side of the boat, above the boat's hull – it keeps the water out of the shell of the boat when conditions become a bit rough (rowers sit between the gunwales, and the riggers are attached to them)

H

half pressure an instruction given by the cox to the crew to use 50% pressure

hands off reaction from a teenager rower when offered a hug by a parent at an event

hands on a command to the crew as they get ready to lift the boat

head a race in which the boats race a fixed course at timed intervals, held in the winter months

heat race leading up to the final in regattas, where one or more boats will go through to the next round

heat for a final at regattas, if there are fewer boats entered into an event than there are lanes, the boats will race each other before the final in order to allocate the lanes in the final – the winning crew has the lane with the best advantage

hold it up an instruction given by the cox to the crew to put blades in the water at an angle to stop the boat abruptly

hot seating when two crews have to share the same boat at a regatta and immediately swap without taking the boat out of the water (or switching seats with your fellow parent during an event, whilst they dash to the loo!)

I

indoor rowing competitions competitions held on ergo machines where the competitors race a fixed distance or time

J

jelly beans snack that can be eaten at the start line for an extra burst of energy

judge there are varying levels of these depending on the size of the event

junior maiden event an event for J15 and above where the crews have not won any qualifying events

K

kit bag essential for any rower – it often seems to be laden with wet kit, old food and 'rank' water bottles!

L

lanes parallel channels used in regattas to mark the bounds for different boats in a race.

lie-ins a thing of the past – waking up because you have had enough sleep

lines/steering wires the ropes that the cox holds to control the rudder

M

marshal a race official – there are many marshals at events, each responsible for some part of the safety and smooth running of the event

marshalling the process of getting to the start of the race – if a crew misses their slot they may not be allowed to race

megaphone what most parents do not need, but all umpires do

N

National Schools (Nat Schools) one of the main rowing events in the summer, open to clubs as well as schools in the appropriate age groups

not rowed out when a crew has failed to complete the course at an event

novice name given to rowers in their first season at a club

novice events events in which the competitors have not won a final at previous events

numbering of seats from front to back (bow to stern), except number 1 is called bow and number 2, 4 or 8 (depending on the size of the boat) is called the stroke

O

oct/octuple a sculling boat with eight rowers using two blades each

official warning a penalty given to a crew for an infringement of the Rules of Racing, or the Guide to Safe Practice in Rowing at an Event (two official warnings means disqualification)

P

paddle rowing with enough strength to move the boat – often used at the start of a session or when winding down; also the part of the blade on which clubs paint their colours

pair a sweeping boat with two rowers and one blade each

patient waiting and not rushing up the slide; or remaining calm and biting your tongue when your rower starts moaning!

PB (personal best) term used to describe your rower's fastest ergo times (shaving a second off an ergo time is a much bigger deal than it sounds)

pieces not designer women's wear separates! Used during training to practise for competitions where the crews row using specific commands for pressure, rate, time or distance or all of these e.g. practice is broken down into 'pieces', such as two minute pieces, four 10 minute pieces etc.

pogi weird looking gloves used by some rowers to keep their hands warm in artic conditions

powerhouse a term used to describe the strongest members of the crew, usually sitting in the middle seats of the boat

PP how your rower might describe a pushy parent

processional a race in which the crews set off in order down the course, with the fastest times through to the next round

puddle the hole the blade makes in the water

push a sudden burst of power during a race

push and shove what is needed to get a rower out of bed when it is raining, snowy or windy at 5am (you have been preparing the picnic for an hour already!)

pyramid rowing a training drill in which the cox calls out increasing power strokes in counts of 10 and then decreases them again in the same way

Q
quad a sculling boat with four rowers with two blades each – usually coxed

R
race assistant a race official who holds the boat into place at the stake boat – they usually lie down to do this
race plan plan of how to row a race, with a start, middle and an end
race rhythm the rhythm that the rowers move to in the middle part of the race, using a set rate to keep a consistent boat speed – this rhythm will carry them through to the sprint at the end of the race (if the rowers are not moving to the same rhythm, the boat will not be working to best effect)
recovery the time between the end of one stroke and the start of the next
recovery period the first two hours after an event or training, when refuelling with fluid and food is vital
red flag flag that indicates 'stop!'
regatta side by side racing, often several heats culminating in a final.
repechage (not a form of French cheese!) a race for those boats that came second in heats to gain a place through to either the semi-final or the final, depending on the number of boats in the category
ribbon essential accessory to be worn around the wrists or woven through hair at main events
rigger a metal bracket on the side of the boat to support the blade (unlike in a traditional rowing boat that uses rollocks) – these lengthen the wingspan and increase the power of the stroke, so the boat moves faster
rigger jigger a small spanner (10mm or 13mm) and essential kit – often left in pockets of trackies and later found at the bottom of the washing machine drum
rigging adjusting parts of the shell of the boat (e.g. tracks, sliding seats, etc.) in order to suit the rowers
rolling start start used at start of head races and processionals where boats reach the start line at full speed
rowing cycle the full series of movements that make up the rowing action.
rushing the slide poor technique in which the rower comes to the catch from recovery too fast, causing momentum against the flow of the boat (stern check)

S

sax board or **gunwales** the top edge of the boat onto which the riggers are attached

scratch crew a group of rowers who have not rowed together before

sculling rowing with two blades

seat racing multiple races in different configurations or matrices to find the fastest boats – there is only one winning solution (the rowing equivalent of Sudoku)

single a sculling boat with one rower and two blades

skying poor technique in which the blades are too high off the water

slide the movement of the seat during the stroke cycle

sling a folding boat stand or trestle

sling and dump the action used by rowers when depositing their wet kit bags at the front door after a session!

split the average time to complete 500m on an ergo

spoon the part of the blade that goes in the water. It differs in shape and size depending on the type of blade

square blades the position of the blade just before it enters the water – if you place square blades in the water it will stop the boat (this is called 'holding up')

stake boat is the boat rowers line up against at the start of a regatta

starting positions position of the boats at the start of a race, with the bows facing down the course and the boat lined up straight – the boat is held at the stake boat by a racing assistant

start line in head races, the line that boats will line up to and cross at the start of the race – the race is timed from when they row across the time line

stern the back of the boat – i.e. the last part past the finishing line

stern check abrupt deceleration of a boat, felt in larger boats when the rowers are out of time with each other so that the momentum of the rowers sends the boat in the opposite direction against the forward motion of the boat (it gives a sensation similar to whiplash and is felt most at the stern by the cox)

stop a crew action taken by an umpire by raising a white flag, naming the crew and giving the command 'stop'

stop a race action taken by an umpire by ringing a bell, raising a red flag and giving the command 'stop'

stretcher/footplate the part of the boat with the shoes for the feet

stretcher needed by parents mid afternoon after very early start!

stride the cruising speed of the boat when at full power – rowers talk about 'settling into their stride' meaning that the stroke rate lowered after a sudden burst or a racing start

stroke the name for the rower setting the pace of the boat in the back seat at the stern; also refers to the complete rowing stroke

stroke blade the blade held on the right of the body – it has a red stripe on it near the handle

stroke rate the number of times the blades enter the water per minute – the higher the stroke rate the faster the boat is travelling

stroke side when the rowing blade is on the right of the rower

sweeping rowing with one blade as part of a crew (rowers do not tend to start sweeping until they are fully grown)

swim test a safety test carried out before rowers can go out on the water to ensure they are competent swimmers. They swim wearing clothes on top of their swimming costumes.

T

tap a light stroke to manoeuvre the boat.

tapering down when the training schedule is easing off before a major event

taping the riggers wrapping the riggers in special boat tape so that the water from waves hits this tape and bounces back out rather than into the boat – used in adverse weather conditions to prevent the boat from taking on too much water

the 2k dreaded ergo test – the make or break of many selections

three quarters pressure an instruction to the crew from a cox meaning use 75% power

Tideway the part of the Thames in London between Putney and Mortlake

time line line that boats pass at the beginning of head races

time trials trials in which rowers compete in various combinations (either in singles or doubles/pairs or fours/quads) for places in boats

to waist a command given to the crew to hold the boat by the sax board and to lift the boat to waist level

to shoulder a command given to the crew to lift the boat to shoulder height and rest the sax board onto shoulders

tuck in an instruction from coach to crew to get closer to the bank (or suck in the abdominal muscles when standing alongside young Olympic rowers in their Lycra)

trackies essential part of any rower's wardrobe, to be worn as low as possible

U

umpire the person who, ultimately, has the final say as to whether the race has been undertaken according to the rules

V

voice something that the cox has to have in abundance and what parents lose after bellowing too loudly at events

W

washing out instruction to crew from overworked rowing parents after an event, when faced with mountains of wet washing ready to be dried

washing up a tiresome job at the end of the meal that always causes arguments!

wash out when the blade handles are pushed down rather than along at the end of the stroke causing the blades to lift from the water

wash up meeting meeting of the coaches of the rowers involved in GB selection to assess the performance of the individuals and to work out crews – they also look at the times that have been achieved and set the standard for subsequent trials

white flag flag that means 'move!' and sometimes 'stop' to a particular crew; also used at the end of a race to indicate approval of the race

winding down decreasing the stroke rate to bring the boat to a stop.

winding it up increasing the stroke rate until the finish line

Y

you don't and won't understand the most common answer to any question about rowing

Z

zzzzzz the noise made by some spectators mid afternoon whilst sitting too comfortably in their folding chairs at an event

You know you have gone too far

You know when you have gone to far as a rowing parent when:

- waking at 7am on weekends seems like a lie-in
- you have taken to jogging around the riverbank in your Lycra in order to get a better view of what is going on at training sessions all in the name of fitness
- you now refer to your child's coach as 'our coach' and their crew as 'our crew'
- your child's club's website is your default setting on your internet search engine
- you have the rowing club's head coach's telephone number saved on speed dial on your mobile phone
- you know more about the new British Rowing points system than 'your' coach
- you know all the GB ergo cut-off times
- you start to give instructions to your rower in multiples of 3 – starting from …'
- your washing machine is on daily, regardless of the demand, and only at 30 degrees
- you are no longer invited out for lunch at weekends as you are either at a regatta or head or preparing for one
- you take the wrong turn off the M4 and end up at Dorney when you are travelling to Heathrow Airport.
- you start dreaming about rowing
- you write a book about rowing

Secret diary of a rowing slave

TIME 7.30 am
DATE 1 January
VENUE Sitting at kitchen table
AIR TEMPERATURE Chilly
STATUS Rough
HAIR Tousled
CAFFEINE Needing more

Have decided that need to be more organised for rowing this coming year, and have jotted down my MUST HAVES!

1) Folding chair – Obtainable from petrol stations or an upmarket version from camping stores at twice the price. Wacky designs will not be acceptable to your rower and are not as cool as you thought.

2) Essential sunglasses – The larger the better. They hide a multitude of sins ie bags, a lack of make up and tears of joy and despair.

3) Wellies – Absolutely essential for muddy wet days (of which there will be many). Hunter wellies in your favourite colour will cut quite a dash.

4) Sun cream – DON'T make the mistake that this is for SUNNY days!! 8 hours by the river in a force 8 gale is like having your face rubbed with sand paper.

5) Binoculars – Can prevent you cheering madly for wrong crew as they row past.

6) Newspaper – The newspaper of the day to be read and reread in the long gaps between your rowers races. Useful for hiding your face when asleep!

7) Picnic bag – Preferably oilskin and water proof. Extra points for cool, funky Cath Kidston design.

8) Hat and Gloves – Strongly recommend thermal gloves. Forget nice soft kid leather fashion statements as they will be ruined and after many hours by the river you will not be able to feel your fingers. A hat is essential wear in the icy cold wind.

9) Thermal underwear – More practical and warmer than multiple layers.

Notes from your coach

Add you own thoughts or note advice from your rower's coach.

DATE	COMMENT

Notes on nutrition

Add your favourite recipes

RECIPE

_____

_____

_____

_____

_____

_____

RECIPE

_____

_____

_____

_____

_____

RECIPE

_____

_____

_____

_____

_____

SNACK IDEAS

_____

_____

_____

_____

_____

Your rower's events record

DATE	EVENT	POSITION

DATE	EVENT	POSITION

DETAILS OF THE LOCAL EVENTS list the events that your club or school attends			
Event	**Venue**	**Postcode/GPS ref**	**Dogs**

Wellies	Paths for bikes	Facilities

Acknowledgements

We would like the thank the following:

Ryan Demaine Director of Rowing at HSOBC for his support and advice
Katie Greves, GB Olympic Rower for her foreword
All members of HSOBC
British Rowing for their support
Juliet Wilson MSc Nutritional Medicine, SENr
Emma Brown - cox for WJ18 8
Isobel Gillan for her enduring patience. She has now left the country...

Joe Blasko - coach St Ignatius High School, USA for use of his quote
Sue Brown, Express Boat Club and regular FISA World Master
    medal winner for use of her quote
Joe Clinard - for use of his quote. He is a 90 year old rower who holds current
    world records.
JJ Forster - Olympic rower and coach Georgetown Rowing Association, USA for
    use of his quote
Quotes from *A Lifetime in a Race* by Matthew Pinsent, published by Ebury Press.
    Reprinted by permission of The Ramdon House Group Ltd
Quotes from *A Red Rose Crew* by Daniel Boyne published by Lyons Press. Quotes
    from *True Blue: The Oxford Boat Race Mutiny* by Daniel Topolski and Patrick
    Robinson, published by Bantam Books. Reprinted by permission of
    The Ramdom House Group Ltd
Quotes from *Wanted - Rowing Coach* by Brad Alan Lewis. Printed by Shark Press.

The River and Rowing Museum, Henley on Thames, for use of facts from
    their website
British Olympic Association for use of facts from their website
Furnivall Sculling Club for use of facts from their website
London Youth Rowing for use of facts from their website
National Schools Regatta for use of facts from their website
The Boat Race for use of facts from their website.

'I watch them carefully, as always, searching for a sign of mental weakness. But there was none. Every man was coping well with the hardship, each one of them locked into his task. But it is one thing to practise and quite another to race. And the trouble is, you never know who, on the day, will find it within his soul to give more than he has ever given before. It takes a kind of madness to compete like that, because of the will power and the ego, and his loyalty. And whilst some men have it, others have yet to find it.' DANIEL TOPOLSKI AND PATRICK ROBINSON, *TRUE BLUE: THE OXFORD BOAT RACE MUTINY*, BANTAM BOOKS, 1989